PLAY FOR ALL

SAFETY FIRST CHECKLIST®

The Site Inspection System for Play Equipment

Sally McIntyre
Susan M. Goltsman
Lowell Kline

Illustrations by:
Mimi Vreeland
Paulette Schafir

Desktop Publishing by:
Voltaire Tinana
Catherine Candee

Distributed by:
National Safety Council
444 North Michigan Avenue
Chicago, IL 60611

Published by:
MIG Communications
1802 Fifth Street
Berkeley, CA 94710
(510) 845-0953

Copyright ©1989, MIG Communications
1802 Fifth Street, Berkeley, CA 94710, USA, (510) 845-0953

Printed in the United States of America

Library of Congress Catalog Card Number: 89–91774
Main Entry Under Title:

Safety First Checklist: The Site Inspection System for Play Equipment

1. Safety Standards
I. McIntyre, Sally

2. Play and Playgrounds
II. Goltsman, Susan M.

3. Environmental Design
III. Kline, Lowell V.

ISBN 0–944661–02–5

ABOUT THE AUTHORS

Sally McIntyre, RTR

Sally McIntyre is a manager of the play environments assessment division of Moore Iacofano Goltsman and is program coordinator for PLAE, Inc. She has over ten years of experience in providing direct service to children with and without disabilities. For the past five years, her work has focused on the integration of children of all abilities through play opportunities and proper environmental design. She specializes in staff training, environmental assessments for safety and access and resource development for play programs. She has published a number of articles on creative play, integration, and safety in professional journals. Her current work includes: furthering the goals of PLAY FOR ALL by promoting safety and play value in children's environments, coordinating projects which transfer the PLAE program model to municipal recreation programs, and editing the *PLAY FOR ALL News*. She serves on the curriculum advisory committee for the Department of Recreation and Leisure Studies at San Francisco State University. She holds a degree in Recreation Administration with an emphasis on Therapeutic Recreation. Sally is a registered recreation therapist

Susan Goltsman, ASLA

Susan Goltsman is a partner with Moore Iacofano Goltsman and is a co-founder and Director of PLAE, Inc. For the past fifteen years, she has been creating programs and special environments that promote the development of children. She has been recognized by the National Endowment for the Arts for her work in environmental education and has won the American Planning Association Award for her work with youth. She has received the 1987 Merit Award from the California Parks and Recreation Society for a significant contribution to the field of therapeutic recreation. Susan coordinated the PLAY FOR ALL effort to develop nationwide guidelines for the planning, design and management of outdoor play areas for all children. The PLAY FOR ALL guidelines have been adopted by thousands of organizations and municipalities all over the country. Currently, Susan is directing THE PLAYFUL CITY, a national effort to create guidelines for the development of urban environments in support of children, youth and their families. She serves on a national committee which is creating standards for play equipment in the United States. Susan teaches at Stanford University in the Program on Urban Studies. She is president of the California Council of Landscape Architects and serves on the boards of the United States Chapter of the International Association for the Child's Right to Play and the Center for Childhood. She holds degrees in Landscape Architecture, Interior Design and Environmental Psychology.

Lowell Kline

Lowell Kline holds a Bachelor's degree in Landscape Architecture. He specializes in information systems, installation and training with a focus on computer applications in the fields of design and communications. Lowell serves as a technical writer and consultant at Moore Iacofano Goltsman. He has developed and installed information management systems for park and recreation agencies and trained staff in their use.

ACKNOWLEDGEMENTS

The authors would like to thank the National Safety Council for their review and support, with special thanks to Nina Moroz and Jodey Schonfeld; designer Jay Beckwith for his knowledge of play equipment and expert and generous advice; Bill Montgomery, Superintendent of the Berkeley Parks and Marina Division, and his staff for the opportunity to field test this document; Dr. Seymour Gold for his in-depth research and his friendship; Dr. Fran Wallach and Dr. Arthur Mittelstaedt for their work in the field of safety and play; Paul Hogan for his contribution to the development of safety tools and to the fields of safety and play; Landscape Structures/Mexico Forge and Kompan play equipment companies for permission to use illustrations of their equipment; and Larry Wight and Catherine Candee for their patient assistance in preparing this manuscript.

TABLE OF CONTENTS

WHEN USING THESE CHECKLISTS ...

The authors, publishers, contributors, distributors and others involved in the preparation of this document assume no risk or liability for incidents arising from the application of this information in any way.

Although the information and recommendations contained in this publication have been compiled from sources believed to be reliable, MIG Communications and the National Safety Council make no guaranty as to, and assumes no responsibility for, the correctness, sufficiency, or completeness of such information or recommendations. Other or addditional safety measures may be required under particular circumstances.

This document should not be construed as a substitute for the CPSC guidelines, for official requirements regarding play equipment or for an independent agencies' own design and safety procedures. This document is to be used in conjunction with a comprehensive playground maintenance program.

WHAT IS THE SAFETY FIRST CHECKLIST?

The Safety First Checklist translates the most up-to-date information on playground safety into an easy-to-use playground equipment inspection system.

The checklist is based on the U.S. Consumer Product Safety Commission Guidelines[1] and the PLAY FOR ALL Guidelines[2]. It includes:

- Modular inspection forms for each play element (swings, slides, climbers, etc.)
- A general site survey
- A surfacing evaluation
- Instructions for making playground inspection tools

In addition, each section identifies key questions to help you evaluate and improve play area accessibility for users with special needs.

IS THE CHECKLIST COMPREHENSIVE?

The Safety First Checklist is intended to provide a comprehensive list of potential safety hazards. However, due to limitations of current research information and the possibility of unique and unpredictable hazards, many critical inspection decisions should be made on-site by a trained playground inspector. In addition, some items were too variable to present in a brief checklist format. Some of these include harmful plants (e.g., local toxic species and trees which drop limbs), former site uses (e.g., landfills or locations where hazardous chemicals have been stored or used), etc.

On-going playground safety research will lead to improvements in this Checklist and ultimately in the design of physical environments. For example, current areas of controversy, such as the use of signs, the use of chemical preservatives on play equipment and site adjacencies to freeways and power lines will invariably lead to future revisions of the Checklist. As knowledge in the field of playground safety is always changing, the best protection against play area hazards continues to be a well trained staff.

---

1   U.S. Consumer Product Safety Commission, *A Handbook for Public Playground Safety. Vol. I: General Guidelines for New and Existing Playgrounds. Vol. II: Technical Guidelines for Equipment and Surfacing.* (Washington, D.C.: CPSC 1981).

2   Robin C. Moore, Susan M. Goltsman and Daniel S. Iacofano, *PLAY FOR ALL Guidelines: Planning, Design, and Management of Outdoor Play Settings for All Children. (Berkeley, CA: MIG Communications 1987).*

HOW IS THE CHECKLIST SYSTEM ORGANIZED?

Separate Checklist sections address the overall site, playground surfacing and individual play equipment items (swings, climbers, etc.). The first page of each section includes an illustration or chart. Next, a series of "Yes" or "No" questions in checklist format allow the inspector to assess safety and accessibility factors.

All "NO" answers indicate a potential safety hazard or accessibility issue. If any item on the Checklist is "No", removal or repair of equipment and/or a site element may be necessary. Play area redesign may also be needed.

The final page of each section is designed to serve as a record of problems and recommended actions. As problems are noted, one or more of the following actions should be taken:

1. Immediate repair;
2. Submit a work order for repair or removal;
3. Close the area; or
4. Notify the supervisor.

List problems and recommended actions for improving the safety and accessibility of each item in the "Work Order" box. If "No Hazardous Conditions are Found", mark this box on the Work Order sheet. The illustration on the first page of each section can be used to indicate the location of repairs which have been listed on the work order.

HOW SHOULD THE CHECKLIST BE USED?

To complete a playground inspection, follow the steps described below:

1. Each inspection begins with an overall site assessment using the **Site Safety Survey Section.** Draw a simple sketch of the site on the front of this section in the space provided. If fall zones are inadequate, indicate the distance between equipment items in your sketch. Play area dimensions will be helpful in calculating costs if redesign becomes necessary. Complete the checklist questions and identify corrective actions for any hazards noted on the Work Order Sheet, including those which would improve site access.

2. Complete the **Surfacing Section.** If any questions are answered No, record the recommended corrective actions on the Work Order section of the form or indicate "No Hazardous Conditions Found". **If the play area has no resilient surfacing under equipment, it should be closed immediately.**

3. After assessing the overall site and surfacing conditions, evaluate each piece of **Equipment** in the play area. Select the appropriate Checklist for each item (e.g., swings, tot swings, climbers, slides, etc.). Complete the survey questions for each item. The Checklist is organized so that severe structural instability, lack of adequate fall zones,

excessive equipment height or entrapment is identified immediately. If during the course of the inspection it becomes evident that a particular piece of equipment must be removed, you may wish to stop the inspection of that piece of equipment.

Example 1: A horizontal ladder does not have the appropriate unobstructed fall zone. Field inspections showed that it was free from severe structural deterioration and did not exceed the recommended equipment height. The inspector's conclusion was that this structure needed relocation. In this case, the play area inspector continued the survey to assess if the horizontal ladder would be safe if relocated to an eight-foot fall zone.

Example 2: During the survey, a linked structure was found to have severe wood rot in all vertical supports. The structure was unstable in several areas. It was evident that the structure could not be repaired and must be immediately removed. After completing the first survey question and discovering the poor condition of the equipment, evaluation of this item was discontinued.

4. If any piece of equipment includes ladders or stairways, attach the **Ladder/Stairway** section to the equipment survey. Answer the checklist questions and complete the Work Order Sheet.

5. Evaluate linked structures by completing the **Linked Structure Section** and a section for each play element included in the structure. For example, to evaluate a linked structure which includes a horizontal ladder and a tire swing, select the Linked Structure, Horizontal Ladder, Tire Swing and Ladder/Stairway Sections. Indicate needed improvements on the Work Order Sheet.

6. Although **site-built and community-built structures** are not recommended, they are common in every park district. To evaluate these structures, select the checklist section or a combination of sections which best describes the structure, e.g, Tunnel, Climber, Linked Structure, etc. Answer the checklist questions and complete the Work Order Sheet.

HOW OFTEN SHOULD A PLAY AREA BE INSPECTED?

The Checklist is designed as a comprehensive site assessment tool for annual inspections. In addition to annual inspections, regular maintenance inspections should be conducted on a monthly basis. A play area also needs daily inspections to maintain resilient surfacing, remove trash and glass and correct basic maintenance problems, especially those due to vandalism.

A monthly maintenance checklist is available from MIG Communications (1802 Fifth Street, Berkeley, CA 94710, 415-845-0953).

INTRODUCTION

**CAN THE SAFETY FIRST CHECKLIST HELP DOCUMENT
PLAYGROUND MAINTENANCE?**

The Checklist can be easily used to document improvements needed for each play area. Simply create a three-ring binder for each play area and select the appropriate pages from the Checklist. The binder can be divided into four sections: section one is the assessment, section two contains a list of all improvements needed, section three is the record of ongoing maintenance, and section four contains all documents relating to the play equipment and site installation.

Following is a list of definitions which apply to the Checklist.

APPROPRIATE SCALE

Equipment should be selected which allows children to use it safely and successfully. It should match the typical users' chronological and mental age as well as physical ability. The height and complexity of play elements should not exceed ability. For example, if equipment is installed for elementary children and the user population becomes predominately preschool age children over a period of time, the play area design is no longer of an appropriate scale. No guidelines have currently been established for preschool play areas. One may assume, however, that suggested heights should be less than those established for elementary children.

ENTRAPMENT

Head Entrapment – Opening Size: Based on the dimensions of the preschool child's head, it is recommended that openings be smaller than three and larger than nine inches to prevent head entrapment. This exceeds the CPSC guidelines.

Head Entrapment – Opening Shape: The CPSC guidelines allows vertical angles greater than 55 degrees. The current industry trend is to remove angles wherever possible. No angle less than 55 degrees should be present in play equipment.

Finger Entrapment: If a child's finger becomes caught in the equipment while they are in motion, it can result in finger loss. Therefore, no openings larger than 3/8" and smaller than 1" should be present on play equipment.

FALL ZONE

All equipment over 30 inches high should have an unobstructed fall zone of resilient surfacing which extends eight feet around it on all sides. Care must be taken to ensure that hard surfaces such as concrete or asphalt do not intrude upon equipment fall zones. Loose surfacing borders and pathways must be located outside of equipment fall zones. For swings, a fall zone distance equal to two times the height of the swing crossbeam should be provided both in front of and behind the equipment. For example, if a swing crossbeam was the maximum recommended height of 8', a 16' foot fall zone should be provided to the front and back of the swings measured from the swing seat location.

DEFINITIONS

MAXIMUM EQUIPMENT HEIGHTS

The following equipment heights are the maximum recommended for elementary age children:

Balance	24"
Bars – Turning	54" (minimum 38")
Bars – Chinning	6' (minimum 38")
Bars – Parallel	48" (minimum 36")
Climber	6'
Chain Climber	6'
Horizontal Ladder	8'
Linked Structure	8'
Moving Bridges	56" to bridge surface
Play House	6' exterior height (minimum 4' interior height)
Ring Trek	8'
Site Built Equipment	6'
Slides	6'
Slides – Bannister	66"
Slides – Firepole	64"
Slides – Tunnels	6'
Swings	8'
Tot Swings	8'

NONCLIMBABLE ENCLOSURE

Any deck over 30" in height should be surrounded by a non-climbable enclosure 38" high. Equipment manufacturers usually accomplish this by installing a solid panel of wood, plastic or metal or a row of vertical slats which are under 3" apart on these decks.

DEFINITIONS

PROTRUSION

The CPSC guidelines allows objects to protrude from structures so long as they are of a minimum size and length. Manufacturers now exceed these guidelines and have removed nearly all protrusions. It is recommended that no element protrude from a structure in any direction which might entrap a child's clothing, cause a child to loose his balance or pose a potential impact hazard.

RESILIENT SURFACING

All play equipment over 30" high must be installed over an eight foot fall zone of resilient surfacing material. (For swing fall zone, see FALL ZONE above.) Since falls are the major cause of serious playground injuries, the goal is to reduce the impact of these accidents. A head first fall from the highest point of the equipment onto the play area surface should result in a impact of 200 g's or less.

Many kinds of resilient surfaces are available. They include sand, wood chips, chopped tire, and synthetic mats. Loose surfacing materials should be installed at a 12" depth throughout the play area (6" for chopped tire).

Manufactured surfaces should be guaranted by the manufacturer to meet the 200 g criteria for the height of equipment used in the play area. This guarantee should become part of the agency's permanent documentation of the play area.

All resilient surfaces require regular maintenance. Loose materials must be raked to keep a 12" depth throughout the play area and to remove trash and glass. Mats must be swept free of glass, cleaned periodically and examined to ensure that it is firmly attached with no exposed hardware. Grass, dirt, pea gravel, concrete and asphalt are never appropriate fall surfaces for play equipment areas.

In addition to a tape measure and ruler, there are a few tools which will be needed in order to evaluate play equipment for potential safety hazards. These can be easily assembled from readily available materials.

GENERAL SAFETY TOOLS

The following three tools are used to measure head and finger entrapment areas. They will be used for the inspection of all play equipment.

Head Entrapment – Opening Shape

Materials Needed:

> Scissors
> Foamcore Board
> Pen
> X-Acto Knife
> Pattern 'A'

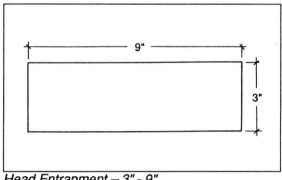

Head Entrapment Angle – 55˚

1. Enlarge Pattern 'A' 164% (or 128% twice) on a photocopy machine so that the resulting paper is 11" x 17". Cut out the triangular arc pattern.

2. Place the pattern on a piece of foamcore board. Trace around the pattern.

3. Cut out the foamcore shape with the X-Acto knife. Label the shape "Head Entrapment Angle – 55°".

4. Use this template to gauge whether or not an angle is less than 55°. If it is, it constitutes a head entrapment hazard.

Head Entrapment – Opening Size

Materials Needed:

> Foamcore Board
> Pen
> Ruler
> X-Acto Knife

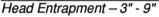

Head Entrapment – 3" - 9"

1. Using the pen and ruler, draw a 9" x 3" rectangle on the foamcore board.

INSPECTION TOOL KIT

2.   Cut out the rectangle using the X-Acto knife. Label the shape "Head Entrapment – 3" - 9".

3.   Use this form to determine whether or not an opening is a head entrapment. If either the 3" or the 9" side of the rectangle fits into an opening in play equipment, this opening presents a potential head entrapment.

Finger Entrapment

Materials Needed:

   1" diameter dowel
   3/8" diameter dowel
   Saw
   Sand Paper
   Ruler
   Pen

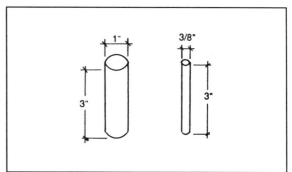

1.   Using the ruler, measure a 3" length on the 1" and 3/8" dowels. Cut the dowels with the saw.

3/8" & 1" dowels

2.   Sand the ends of the dowels using sand paper.

3.   Label the tools "Finger Entrapment - 3/8" – 1".

4.   If any gap in play equipment is large enough for the 3/8" dowel to pass through but not larger than the 1" dowel, this gap is a potential finger entrapment.

SLIDE SAFETY TOOL

This slide tool is used to measure the angle of the slide exit zone.

Exit Zone Angle

Materials Needed:

   Scissors
   Foamcore Board
   Pen
   X-Acto Knife
   Pattern 'B'

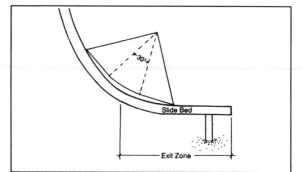

Slide Exit Zone Angle – 30°

1.   Enlarge Pattern 'B' 164% (or 128% twice) on a photocopy machine so that the resulting paper is 11" x 17". Cut out the triangular arc pattern.

2.   Place the pattern on a piece of foamcore board. Trace around the pattern.

3.   Cut out the foamcore shape with the X-Acto knife. Label the shape "Slide Exit Zone Angle – 30°".

4.   Use this template to gauge whether or not the angle of the slide exit zone is at least 30°. To use the Exit Zone Angle, place it vertically on the slide at the point where the slope of the slide bed curves to form a level exit zone. If both sides of the tool come in contact with the slide bed leaving a gap between the tool and the bed, the angle of the slide exit zone is too abrupt and poses a hazard.

SPIRAL SLIDE TOOLS

The following tools are used to assess spiral slide safety. These tools may not be necessary if the maximum vertical drop of the slide chute (height of the spiral) is over 64". (See Section 20A, Spiral Slide Safety, Question 5.)

Curve Gauge

Materials Needed:

   Scissors
   Foamcore Board
   Pen
   X-Acto Knife
   Pattern 'C'

1.   Photocopy Pattern 'C' and cut it out. The pattern does not need to be enlarged.

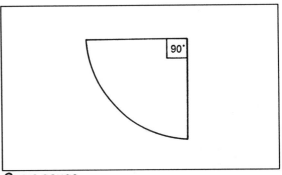
Curve gauge

2.   Place the pattern on a piece of foamcore board. Trace around the pattern.

3.   Cut out the foamcore shape with the X-Acto knife. Label the shape "Spiral Slide Curve Gauge".

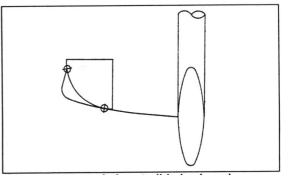
Curve gauge and abrupt slide bed angle

4. To use the Curve Gauge, place the curved edge against the angle formed by the slide chute rail and the slide bed. If both corners of the curved edge make contact with the slide in this position, the slide has an ABRUPT ANGLE. If only one corner of the curved edge makes contact with the slide in this position, the slide has a CONTINUOUS CURVE. This tool is used in Section 20A, Spiral Slide Safety, Question 7.

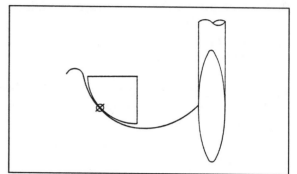

Curve gauge and continuous curve slide bed angle

Abrupt Angle Slide Rule

Materials Needed:

> Scissors
> Foamcore Board
> Crescent Board
> 6" Protractor
>   (such as C-THRU #376)
> String
> Small (approx. 1/2") Torpedo
>   Fishing Weight
> Pen
> Ruler
> X-Acto Knife
> Multi-purpose Cement
>   (e.g. Elmer's StickAll)

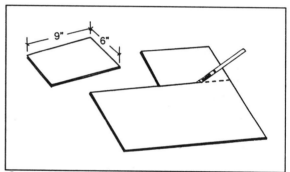

Crescent board for abrupt angle slide rule

1. Using an X-Acto knife, cut two 9" x 6" rectangles out of crescent board.

2. Cut the following out of foamcore board using an X-Acto knife: one 6" x 6" square; one 2" x 6" rectangle; and one 10" x 1" rectangle.

3. Round both 1" ends of the 10" x 1" foamcore rectangle. This piece is the sliding scale.

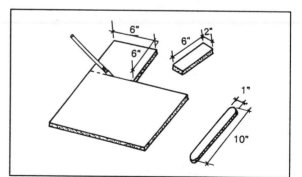

Foamcore for abrupt angle slide rule

4. Glue the two pieces of foamcore board (6" x 6" square and 2" x 6" rectangle to one of the 9" x 6" crescent board rectangles. Leave a 1" gap between the foamcore pieces on the crescent board rectangle as indicated in the illustration. The 10" x 1" foamcore strip (sliding scale) should fit snugly in this channel and be moveable up and down.

5. Being careful to avoid the sliding scale, glue the second 9" x 6" crescent board rectangle to the back of the assembly. The sliding scale should still slide up and down.

6. Using a pen and ruler, mark off the sliding scale (1" x 10" foamcore board strip) by ½" increments on both sides. Label the 1" mark increments. See the illustration below.

7. In the center of the sliding scale at the 9 ½" increment mark, draw an "X". Repeat on the other side of the sliding scale. This "X" will represent the point in space used in measuring the spiral slide radius.

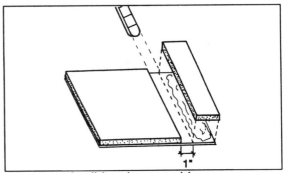

Abrupt angle slide rule assembly

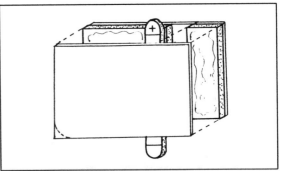

Abrupt angle slide rule assembly

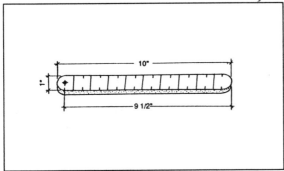

Slide rule sliding scale

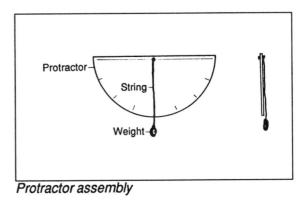

Protractor assembly

8. From the bottom corner of the rectangle assembly farthest from the sliding scale, measure 1½" on each side and mark these two points. Cut off this corner between the two marks (refer to illustration).

9. Cut a piece of string approximately 4½" long. Tie the fishing weight securely to one end. Tie the opposite end of the string through the center hole of the protractor. The string should remain long enough so that the weight will not interfere with reading the protractor.

10. Glue the protractor to the center of the 9" x 6" rectangle. When the 9" edge of the rectangle is held flat on a level surface, the weight should read 90° and should swing freely on the string.

11. Label the tool "Abrupt Angle Slide Rule".

12. To use the tool, see Section 20A, Spiral Slide Safety, Question 8.

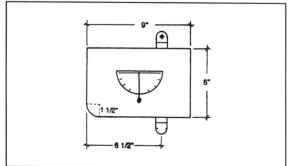

Abrupt angle slide rule

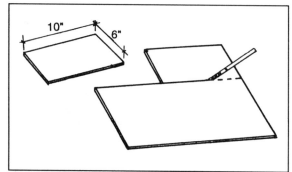

Crescent board for continuous curve slide rule

Continuous Curve Slide Rule

Materials Needed:

    Scissors
    Foamcore Board
    Crescent Board
    6" Protractor (such as C-THRU #376)
    String
    Small (approx. ½") Torpedo Fishing Weight
    Pen
    Ruler
    X-Acto Knife
    Household Cement

1. Using an X-Acto knife, cut two 10" x 6" rectangles out of crescent board.

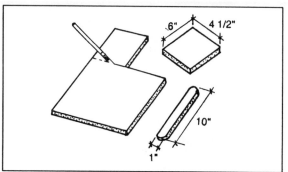

Foamcore for continuous curve slide rule

2. Cut the following out of foamcore board using an X-Acto knife: two 4½" x 6" rectangles and one 10" x 1" rectangle.

3. Round both 1" ends of the 10" x 1" foamcore core rectangle. This piece is the sliding scale.

4. Using household cement, glue the two foamcore board rectangles to one of the 10" x 6" crescent board rectangles. Leave a 1" gap between the foamcore pieces in the center of the crescent board rectangle as indicated in the illustration. The 10" x 1" foamcore strip (sliding scale) should fit snugly in this channel and be moveable up and down.

5. Being careful to avoid the sliding scale, glue the second 10" x 6" crescent board rectangle to the back of the assembly. The sliding scale should still slide up and down.

6. Using a pen and ruler, mark off the sliding scale (1" x 10" foamcore board strip) by 1/2" increments on both sides. Label the 1" mark increments. See the illustration.

7. In the center of the sliding scale at the 9 1/2" increment mark, draw an "X". Repeat on the other side of the sliding scale. This "X" will represent the point in space used in measuring the spiral slide radius.

8. Cut a piece of string approximately 4½" long. Tie the fishing weight securely to one end. Tie the opposite end of the string through the center hole of the protractor. The string should remain long enough so that the weight will not interfere with reading the protractor.

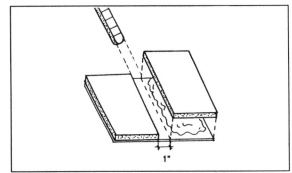

Continuous curve slide rule assembly

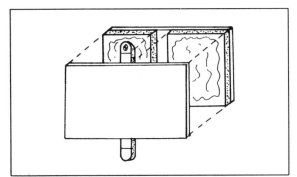

Continuous curve slide rule assembly

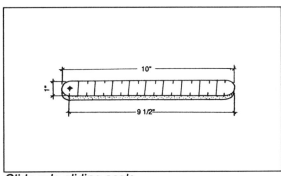

Slide rule sliding scale

9. Glue the protractor to the center of the 10" x 6" rectangle. When the 10" edge of the rectangle is held flat on a level surface, the weight should read 90° and should swing freely on the string.

10. Label the tool "Continuous Curve Slide Rule".

11. To use the tool, see Section 20A, "Spiral Slide Safety," Question 12.

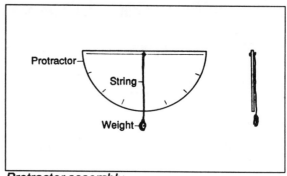

Protractor assembly

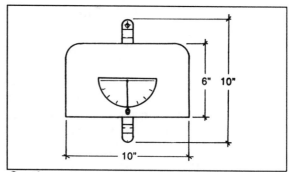

Continuous curve slide rule

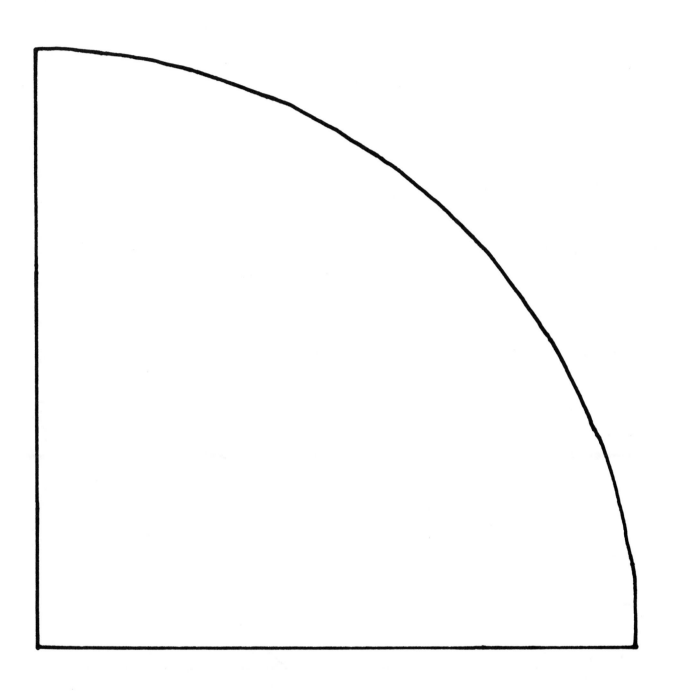

Pattern 'A'
Head Entrapment Angle – 55°

Enlarge approximately 164% (or 128% twice)
The sides of the angle should be 12"

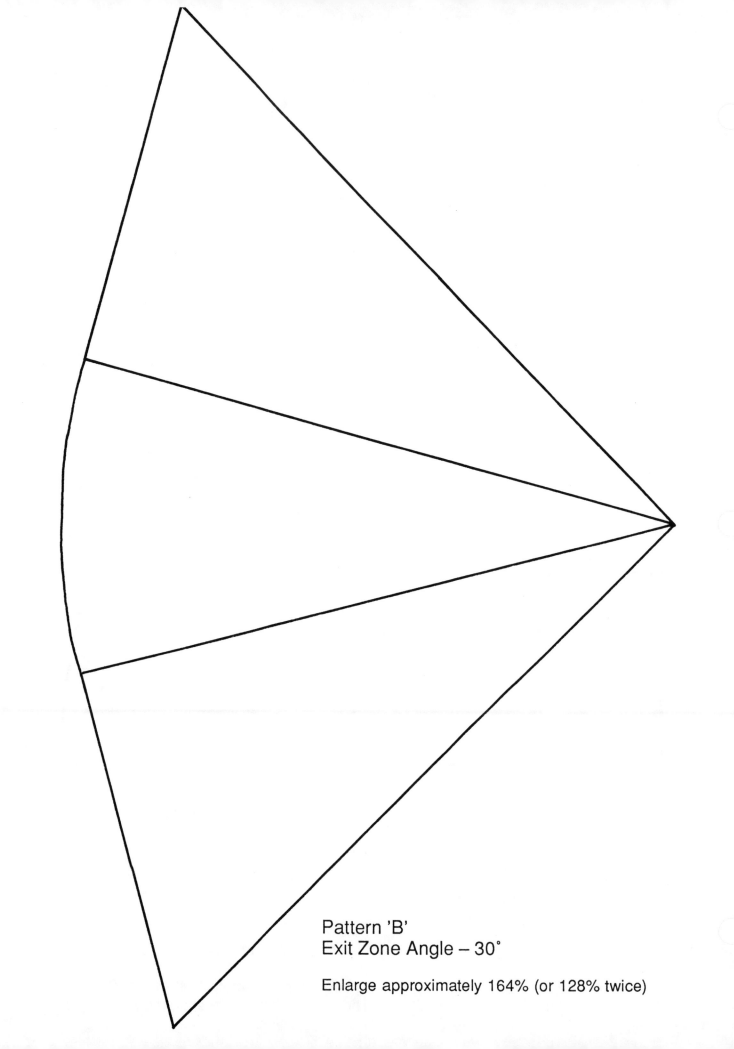

Pattern 'B'
Exit Zone Angle – 30˚

Enlarge approximately 164% (or 128% twice)

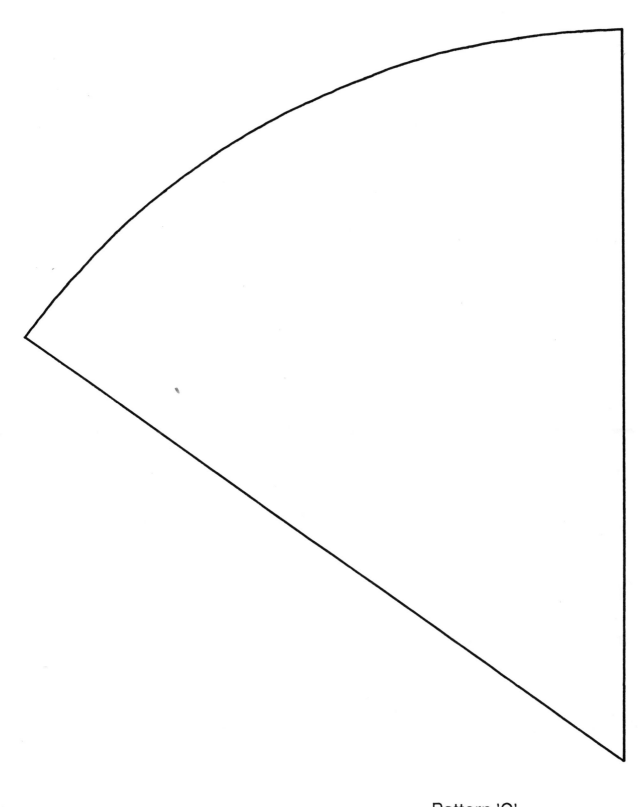

Pattern 'C'
Curve Gauge

No enlargement is necessary

PARK NAME _____

ADDRESS _____

DATE OF INSPECTION _____

INSPECTOR _____

OWNERS _____

HOURS _____ SUPERVISED _____ UNSUPERVISED _____

NO. OF HOURS OF MAINTENANCE PER WEEK _____

DIMENSIONS OF PLAY AREA _____

LAYOUT: Please draw in location of each element.
Scale used: 1 inch = _____ feet　　　　　　　　　(4 squares/inch)

PARK NAME	DATE OF INSPECTION	INSPECTOR

If any of these items is answered NO, correct the problem immediately.

GENERAL CONSIDERATIONS

1. Is the site clean and well maintained?   Yes   No   N/A

2. The site contains:

    - ❑ Manufactured play equipment
    - ❑ Site built play equipment
    - ❑ Shade trees
    - ❑ Pathways
    - ❑ Parking
    - ❑ Bike racks
    - ❑ Benches
    - ❑ Shaded seating
    - ❑ Water element
    - ❑ Water fountain
    - ❑ Barbeque/picnic area

    - ❑ Dramatic play area
    - ❑ Sports fields
    - ❑ Hard surface for ball play
    - ❑ Storage
    - ❑ Grass area
    - ❑ Night lighting
    - ❑ Public restrooms
    - ❑ Public telephones
    - ❑ Trash recepticals
    - ❑ Community center
    - ❑ _____
    - ❑ _____

3. Can the playground be reached safely by bicycle or on foot (unobstructed pathways, stop signs or stop lights)?   Yes   No   N/A

4. Are automobile parking and driving areas separated from pedestrian and waiting zones?   Yes   No   N/A

5. Is the playground readily visible from the street?   Yes   No   N/A

6. Is perimeter fencing provided?   Yes   No   N/A

7. Is the fencing in good condition, with no gap 3" or greater between the fence and the surfacing?   Yes   No   N/A

8. Is the fencing difficult to climb?   Yes   No   N/A

9. Are there informational signs about the use of the park and equipment?   Yes   No   N/A

PARK NAME

DATE OF INSPECTION

INSPECTOR

10. Is sign information presented in both graphic and written forms?   Yes   No   N/A

11. Is the use of culverts (concrete pipes or tunnels) as play equipment avoided except when the pipe is covered with dirt?   Yes   No   N/A

12. Is an 8' fall zone provided for each piece of equipment except where specified in this checklist (e.g., swings, hill slides, etc.)?   Yes   No   N/A

13. Is the pathway located outside of the equipment fall zone?   Yes   No   N/A

14. Is the pathway free from loose surfacing material?   Yes   No   N/A

15. Is the play area, pathway and entranceway free from trip hazards (protruding roots, rocks or obstacles, or pavement height differentials)?   Yes   No   N/A

16. Is there adequate drainage (no puddling or area washed away) in the play area?   Yes   No   N/A

17. Do the restrooms appear safe (e.g., an open design allows sight lines under the structure and prevents its use as an overnight shelter)?   Yes   No   N/A

18. Is the area free from other hazards (utility boxes, drainage ditches, drain pipes, sewer covers that can be removed/ vandalized, dumpsters)?   Yes   No   N/A

19. Are trees free from cracked limbs or pointed snags?   Yes   No   N/A

20. Is the use of pesticides/herbicides avoided in the play area?   Yes   No   N/A

21. Is the play area free of vandalism?   Yes   No   N/A

PARK NAME	DATE OF INSPECTION	INSPECTOR

SITE ACCESSIBILITY

22. Is at least one primary entrance usable by persons in wheelchairs?   Yes   No   N/A

23. When the accessible entrance is other than the main entrance, is a sign showing the location of the accessible entrance posted at the main entrance and visible from the sidewalk?   Yes   No   N/A

24. Do gates have a clear opening of 32" when open?   Yes   No   N/A

25. Do gates open at a 90 degree angle?   Yes   No   N/A

26. Are sharp inclines and abrupt changes in level (over 1/4") avoided at entrances?   Yes   No   N/A

27. Does the entrance gate lead to a level platform large enough to be usable by wheelchairs (at least 5'x5')?   Yes   No   N/A

28. Are accessible parking spaces provided and identified by appropriate signage?   Yes   No   N/A

29. Are accessible parking spaces as close as possible to the accessible entrance?   Yes   No   N/A

30. Are an appropriate # of parking spaces provided?   Yes   No   N/A

# SPACES	# ACCESSIBLE	# SPACES	#ACCESSIBLE
1 – 25	1	151 – 200	6
26 – 50	2	201 – 300	7
51 – 75	3	301 – 400	8
76 – 100	4	401 - 500	9
101 - 150	5	501 - 1000	2% of total

31. Are accessible spaces 14 feet wide and lined to provide a 5 foot loading area?   Yes   No   N/A

32. Is there room to get in and out of an automobile at a level surface?   Yes   No   N/A

PARK NAME	DATE OF INSPECTION	INSPECTOR

33. Can individuals in wheelchairs or using braces and crutches reach the entrance without going behind parked cars?   Yes   No   N/A

PATHWAYS

34. Are there clearly defined pathways?   Yes   No   N/A

35. Are pathways at least 48" wide?   Yes   No   N/A

36. Is the slope less than 5%? (1 foot rise in 20 feet.)   Yes   No   N/A

37. Are pathways of a continuing common surface with no steps or abrupt change in level exceeding 1/4"?   Yes   No   N/A

38. Is there a minimum clearance of 8'6" high over pathways?   Yes   No   N/A

39. Are there curb cuts adequate to provide an accessible path of travel?   Yes   No   N/A

40. Are pedestrian ramps or bridges accessible? (Slope less than 1 foot rise in 12 feet (8.33%); handrails provided on both sides of the ramp 32" above the ramp surface and extending 1 foot beyond the top and bottom of the ramp; non-slip surface; level platforms at 30 foot intervals and wherever the ramp changes direction; ramp platforms at least 5 feet x 5 feet; 6 feet of straight clearance at the bottom; 48" wide.)   Yes   No   N/A

PARK NAME	DATE OF INSPECTION	INSPECTOR

SITE FURNISHINGS AND AMENITIES

41. If there are restrooms, are they usable by people in wheelchairs?
(Accessible entrance, large stall (5' x 6'), grab bars, door width 32", door swings outward, toilet seat mounted at 1'8", accessories located for wheelchair access.)

Yes   No   N/A

42. If there are public telephones, is one accessible?
(A maximum height of 48" forward approach or 54" side approach with unobstructed knee and toe space 27" high; height of operator button does not exceed 46.")

Yes   No   N/A

43. If there are drinking fountains, is one accessible?
(Control located within 6" of the front and hand or hand-and-foot operated; easily operated, e.g., hand-operated lever or push bar; bubbler within 6" of front of the water fountain and no higher than 33" above the floor; unobstructed space provided under the fountain 27" high, 30" wide, and 17"-19" deep.)

Yes   No   N/A

44. If there are barbeque grills, is one accessible?
(Unobstructed space provided underneath at least 27" high and a minimum of 18" deep. Grills should be used by a side approach or completely insulated to prevent burns.)

Yes   No   N/A

45. If there are picnic tables, is one accessible?
(Unobstructed space provided underneath at least 27" high and a minimum of 24"-28" deep. A completely unobstructed depth is preferred.)

Yes   No   N/A

46. Is unobstructed space (3'-5') provided to park a wheelchair next to benches?

Yes   No   N/A

SITE RECOMMENDATIONS

PARK NAME

DATE OF INSPECTION

INSPECTOR

Hazards are apparent from this Inspection:

❑ Repair the problem,
❑ Submit a work order,
❑ Barricade or close the area, or
❑ Notify your supervisor.
❑ _____

SITE SAFETY RECOMMENDATIONS

❑ No Hazardous Conditions Found
❑ Removal/Repair Necessary (Prepare Work Order)

WORK ORDER

Item	Action	Date Completed	Time Spent	Cost ($)

SITE ACCESSIBILITY RECOMMENDATIONS

Item	Action	Date Completed	Time Spent	Cost ($)

PARK NAME

DATE OF INSPECTION

INSPECTOR

SURFACING MATRIX

MATERIAL	SAFETY ISSUES	RECOMMENDED DEPTH
I. **ORGANIC LOOSE MATERIAL** (pine bark, bark nuggets, shredded bark, cocoa shell mulch, etc.)	Environmental conditions such as wind, playing action, moisture, freezing temperatures, decomposition, and combining with dirt can reduce fall absorbency; susceptibility to burning; ideal for microorganism growth when wet; problems with wood post deterioration; can get thrown around; spreads outside containment barrier; conceals animal excrement and sharp objects.	12 inches
A. Bark Nuggets	Softness accelerates its decomposition process; some children are allergic to bark dust.	12 inches
B. Wood Chips	Suitability depends on the wood source: coniferous chips are the best because they are not as splintery as hardwood when first spread; pine scent is an added attraction and the pine needles help to make a soft "mat." Softer hardwoods such as sycamore are almost as good.	12 inches
II. **INORGANIC LOOSE MATERIAL** (sand, chopped tire, etc.)	Environmental conditions such as those listed above can reduce fall absorbency; can be aspirated, swallowed, blown, or thrown; spreads outside the containment area; conceals animal excrement and sharp objects.	12 inches
A. Sand	Particles 1/32 inch or less tend to bind together when wet; Particles larger than 3/8 inch can cause serious eye injury when thrown; composition of original stone affects longevity; if used under play equipment, additional sand areas must be provided for play or children will play in fall zone areas creating a hazardous situation. Possible asbestos content.	12 inches
B. Chopped Tire	Can be aspirated, swallowed, or thrown around; spreads outside its containment area; the surface tends to deteriorate with wear and is subject to vandalism; to counteract this, binder material or artificial grass is added; is flammable.	4 - 8 inches
III. **SYNTHETIC COMPACT MATERIALS** (rubber mats, synthetic turf on foam mats, rubber sheeting on foam mats, poured in place urethanes, and rubber compositions)	Must meet 200-G-force rating for potential fall zone; susceptible to vandalism; sharp edges or trip hazards at seams or attachment points; slip resistency; water drainage.	Ranges from 1-6 inches; thickness depends on the equipment height and product resiliency.

PARK NAME

DATE OF INSPECTION

INSPECTOR

If any of these items is answered NO, correct the problem immediately.

1. Is there resilient surfacing under the equipment?
   (Grass,pea gravel, dirt, asphalt and concrete are not
   acceptable)
   **Note: If this question is answered NO, close the play
   area immediately.**

   Yes   No   N/A

2. What type of material?

   ❑ Sand   ❑ Wood chips   ❑ Chopped tire
   ❑ Synthetic mat material
   ❑ Other _____

LOOSE MATERIAL

3. Is loose surfacing material maintained at a 10 – 12 inch
   depth throughout the play area (except chopped tire which
   should be a minimum of 4 – 8 inches deep)?

   Yes   No   N/A

4. Are loose materials free from glass and debris?

   Yes   No   N/A

5. Are the borders of sufficient depth to adequately contain
   12" of loose surfacing material (a border height of 16" is
   suggested)?

   Yes   No   N/A

6. Is the border free from splinters, sharp edges, broken
   boards or protruding nails or bolts?

   Yes   No   N/A

SYNTHETIC COMPACT MATERIAL

7. Name of Product _____ Manufacturer _____.

8. Is the mat complete and intact without serious wear?

   Yes   No   N/A

9. Are the mat hardware and attachment points secure and
   shielded?

   Yes   No   N/A

PARK NAME

DATE OF INSPECTION

INSPECTOR

10. Does a headfirst fall onto the surface from the maximum   Yes   No   N/A
    height of the equipment result in an impact of 200 g's or
    less? (Note: The surfacing manufacturer should provide
    written verification that the surfacing material meets the
    200g criteria. There is also a manufactured testing device
    which will test synthetic mat and loose surfacing materials.
    For information on this testing device contact: Paul Hogan,
    Playground Clearinghouse, 26 Buckwater Rd.,
    Phoenixville, PA 19460, 215-935-1549.)

PARK NAME	DATE OF INSPECTION	INSPECTOR

SURFACING ACCESSIBILITY

11. Is the surfacing material accessible to individuals who use wheelchairs, canes, crutches, walkers or other assistive devices? (See Surfacing Accessibility Matrix below.)   Yes   No   N/A

12. Does the surfacing material or texture change between circulation paths and safety zones?   Yes   No   N/A

13. If a loose surfacing material is used, is access provided through the play equipment border?   Yes   No   N/A

SURFACING ACCESSIBILITY MATRIX

Bark Nuggets	Challenging; requires upper body strength of wheelchair users; ambulatory disabled may find walking difficult.
Wood Chips	Wheelchair accessible once matted down; challenging for ambulatory disabled who may experience balance problems on uneven surfaces.
Sand	Inaccessible to wheelchairs or ambulatory disabled; should not be eliminated from play areas because of its play value.
Chopped Tire	Wheelchair accessible with difficulty; inaccessible for ambulatory disabled who may experience balance problems when walking on this surface.
Synthetic Mat	Accessible.

PARK NAME

DATE OF INSPECTION

INSPECTOR

Hazards are apparent from this inspection:

❑   Repair the problem,
❑   Submit a work order,
❑   Barricade or close the area, or
❑   Notify your supervisor.
❑   _____

SURFACING SAFETY RECOMMENDATIONS

❑   No Hazardous Conditions Found
❑   Removal/Repair Necessary (Prepare Work Order)

WORK ORDER

Item	Action	Date Completed	Time Spent	Cost ($)

SURFACING ACCESSIBILITY RECOMMENDATIONS

Item	Action	Date Completed	Time Spent	Cost ($)

PARK NAME

DATE OF INSPECTION

INSPECTOR

TYPE OF BALANCE EVENT _____

MANUFACTURER _____

Maximum
Height 24"

PARK NAME	DATE OF INSPECTION	INSPECTOR

If any of these items are NO, repair/remove the equipment immediately.

EQUIPMENT CONDITION/HEIGHT/FALL ZONE

1. Is the equipment stable and without severe structural deterioration (e.g., at footings and joints)?   Yes   No   N/A

2. Does the equipment have an 8' obstruction-free fall zone? (If the balance event is not elevated and is installed directly on the ground, dirt or grass may be used as a fall surface. Hard surfaces such as concrete or asphalt are not acceptable.)   Yes   No   N/A

3. Are the heights of balance events 24" or less?   Yes   No   N/A

4. Is the walking surface free from trip hazards?   Yes   No   N/A

ENTRAPMENT

5. Are all openings smaller than 3/8" or greater than 1" to prevent finger entrapment?   Yes   No   N/A

6. Are openings smaller than 3" or larger than 9" to prevent head entrapment?   Yes   No   N/A

GENERAL CONSIDERATIONS

7. Is the equipment complete without missing parts, free of vandalism which would impair safe use, and has no warping or bending of members.   Yes   No   N/A

8. Is the equipment free from pinch or crush points?   Yes   No   N/A

9. Is the equipment free from sharp points, corners, or edges?   Yes   No   N/A

10. Is the equipment free from any protrusions (all nuts and bolts are recessed, fitted with tamper proof locks and the holes plugged)?   Yes   No   N/A

PARK NAME

DATE OF INSPECTION

INSPECTOR

11. Are the tops of concrete footings buried 12" below the ground level?   Yes   No   N/A

12. Is the scale of the equipment appropriate to the size of the users?   Yes   No   N/A

CHAIN/ROPE/CABLE

13. Is rope sound and in good repair?   Yes   No   N/A

14. Is the chain in good condition without significant wear?   Yes   No   N/A

15. Is the chain "proof coil" of 5/0 size with welded links?   Yes   No   N/A

16. Is the cable in good condition without significant wear? Are cable splices and ends free of projecting wires?   Yes   No   N/A

HARDWARE

17. Is all hardware present, securely attached, and without significant wear or evidence of deformation?   Yes   No   N/A

18. Do fasteners and connecting devices require tools to loosen or remove them (i.e., no hex head bolts or nails are used)?   Yes   No   N/A

PARK NAME

DATE OF INSPECTION

INSPECTOR

STRUCTURAL MATERIALS

The structure is made of _____ .

For Wood:

19. Are load bearing members free from rot or insect damage?   Yes   No   N/A

20. Are wood members free from checks more than 24" in length and/or 1/4" in width?   Yes   No   N/A

21. If a wood preservative was used on the structure, list the preservatives name:_____ .

22. Is the wood preservative safe for use in children's play areas?   Yes   No   N/A

23. If a wood preservative was used, has a sealant been applied to treated areas every two years?   Yes   No   N/A

For Metal:

24. If it is steel, is it galvanized or powder coated?   Yes   No   N/A

25. If it is aluminum, is it powder coated or anodized?   Yes   No   N/A

26. Is the equipment free from rust on steel, corrosion on aluminum, or peeling paint?   Yes   No   N/A

For Plastic:

27. Are plastic parts unbroken and without chips or cracks, particularly at joints and connections?   Yes   No   N/A

For Paint:

28. If equipment was painted, was paint without lead used?   Yes   No   N/A

PARK NAME	DATE OF INSPECTION	INSPECTOR

BALANCE EVENT ACCESSIBILITY

29. Is the equipment accessible to individuals with the following disabilities (please check all that apply):   Yes   No   N/A

   ❑ Wheelchair Users   ❑ Cane/Crutch/Walker Users
   ❑ Developmentally Disabled   ❑ Hearing Impaired
   ❑ Visually Impaired   ❑ Emotional/Behavioral Disability

30. Is there a way to make this piece usable by a great number of people with disabilities? (Please specify.)   Yes   No   N/A

   _____

   _____

   _____

   _____

   _____

   _____

31. Can the equipment be adapted without creating a safety hazard for others?   Yes   No   N/A

32. Can a person using a wheelchair, cane, crutches or other assistive device approach the equipment?   Yes   No   N/A

33. Are clear sight lines provided from the equipment to adult supervision areas?   Yes   No   N/A

34. Is the equipment easily understood?   Yes   No   N/A

BALANCE EVENT RECOMMENDATIONS

PARK NAME	DATE OF INSPECTION	INSPECTOR

Hazards are apparent from this inspection:

- ❑ Repair the problem,
- ❑ Submit a work order,
- ❑ Barricade or close the area, or
- ❑ Notify your supervisor.
- ❑ _____

BALANCE EVENT SAFETY RECOMMENDATIONS

- ❑ No Hazardous Conditions Found
- ❑ Removal/Repair Necessary (Prepare Work Order)

WORK ORDER

Item	Action	Date Completed	Time Spent	Cost ($)

BALANCE EVENT ACCESSIBILITY RECOMMENDATIONS

Item	Action	Date Completed	Time Spent	Cost ($)

PARK NAME

DATE OF INSPECTION

INSPECTOR

TYPE OF BAR _____

MANUFACTURER _____

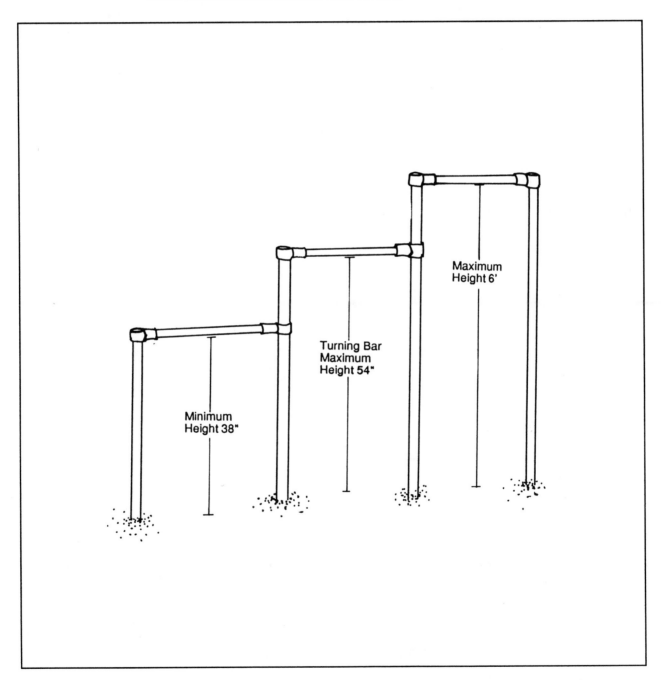

Maximum
Height 6'

Turning Bar
Maximum
Height 54"

Minimum
Height 38"

CHINNING AND TURNING BAR SAFETY
4A

PARK NAME	DATE OF INSPECTION	INSPECTOR

If any of these items are NO, repair/remove the equipment immediately.

EQUIPMENT CONDITION/HEIGHT/FALL ZONE

1. Is the equipment stable and without severe structural deterioration (e.g., at footings and joints)?   Yes   No   N/A

2. Does the bar have an 8' obstruction-free fall zone?   Yes   No   N/A

3. Is the bar height at least 38" and less than 54"(6' for chinning bars)?   Yes   No   N/A

ENTRAPMENT

4. Are all openings smaller than 3/8" or greater than 1" to prevent finger entrapment?   Yes   No   N/A

5. Are openings smaller than 3" or larger than 9" to prevent head entrapment?   Yes   No   N/A

6. Are angles greater than 55° to prevent head entrapment?   Yes   No   N/A

GENERAL CONSIDERATIONS

7. Is the equipment complete without missing parts, free of vandalism which would impair safe use, and has no warping or bending of members.   Yes   No   N/A

8. Is the equipment free from pinch or crush points?   Yes   No   N/A

9. Is the equipment free from sharp points, corners, or edges?   Yes   No   N/A

10. Is the equipment free from any protrusions (all nuts and bolts are recessed, fitted with tamper proof locks and the holes plugged)?   Yes   No   N/A

11. Is the equipment free from suspended cables, wires, or ropes which would allow a rapidly moving child to impact his head or neck?   Yes   No   N/A

PARK NAME	DATE OF INSPECTION	INSPECTOR

12. Is the pole diameter between 1-3/8" and 2-1/2"?	Yes	No	N/A
13. Are the tops of concrete footings buried 12" below the ground level?	Yes	No	N/A
14. Is the scale of the equipment appropriate to the size of the users?	Yes	No	N/A

HARDWARE

15. Is all hardware present, securely attached, and without significant wear or evidence of deformation?	Yes	No	N/A
16. Do fasteners and connecting devices require tools to loosen or remove them (i.e., no hex head bolts or nails are used)?	Yes	No	N/A

STRUCTURAL MATERIALS

The structure is made of _____.

For wood:

17. Are load bearing members free from rot or insect damage?	Yes	No	N/A
18. Are wood members free from checks more than 24" in length and/or 1/4" in width?	Yes	No	N/A

19. If a wood preservative was used on the structure, list the preservatives name:_____.

20. Is the wood preservative safe for use in children's play areas?	Yes	No	N/A
21. If a wood preservative was used, has a sealant been applied to treated areas every two years?	Yes	No	N/A

For Metal:

22. If it is steel, is it galvanized or powder coated?	Yes	No	N/A

PARK NAME	DATE OF INSPECTION	INSPECTOR

23. If it is aluminum, is it powder coated or anodized?   Yes   No   N/A

24. Is the equipment free from rust on steel, corrosion on aluminum, or peeling paint?   Yes   No   N/A

For Plastic:

25. Are plastic parts unbroken and without chips or cracks, particularly at joints and connections?   Yes   No   N/A

For Paint:

26. If equipment is painted, was paint without lead used?   Yes   No   N/A

PARK NAME	DATE OF INSPECTION	INSPECTOR

CHINNING AND TURNING BAR ACCESSIBILITY

27. Is the equipment accessible to individuals with the following disabilities (please check all that apply):　　Yes　　No　　N/A

    ❑ Wheelchair Users   ❑ Cane/Crutch/Walker User
    ❑ Developmentally Disabled   ❑ Hearing Impaired
    ❑ Visually Impaired   ❑ Emotional/Behavioral Disability

28. Is there a way to make this piece usable by a great number of people with disabilities? (Please specify.)　　Yes　　No　　N/A

    _____

    _____

    _____

    _____

    _____

    _____

29. Can the equipment be adapted without creating a safety hazard for others?　　Yes　　No　　N/A

30. Can a person using a wheelchair, cane, crutches or other assistive device approach the equipment?　　Yes　　No　　N/A

31. Are clear sight lines provided from the equipment to adult supervision areas?　　Yes　　No　　N/A

32. Is the equipment easily understood?　　Yes　　No　　N/A

CHINNING BAR RECOMMENDATIONS

4C

PARK NAME	DATE OF INSPECTION	INSPECTOR

Hazards are apparent from this Inspection:

- ❑ Repair the problem,
- ❑ Submit a work order,
- ❑ Barricade or close the area, or
- ❑ Notify your supervisor.
- ❑ _____

CHINNING/TURNING BAR SAFETY RECOMMENDATIONS

- ❑ No Hazardous Conditions Found
- ❑ Removal/Repair Necessary (Prepare Work Order)

WORK ORDER

Item	Action	Date Completed	Time Spent	Cost ($)

CHINNING / TURNING BAR ACCESSIBILITY RECOMMENDATIONS

Item	Action	Date Completed	Time Spent	Cost ($)

PARK NAME

DATE OF INSPECTION

INSPECTOR

MANUFACTURER _____.

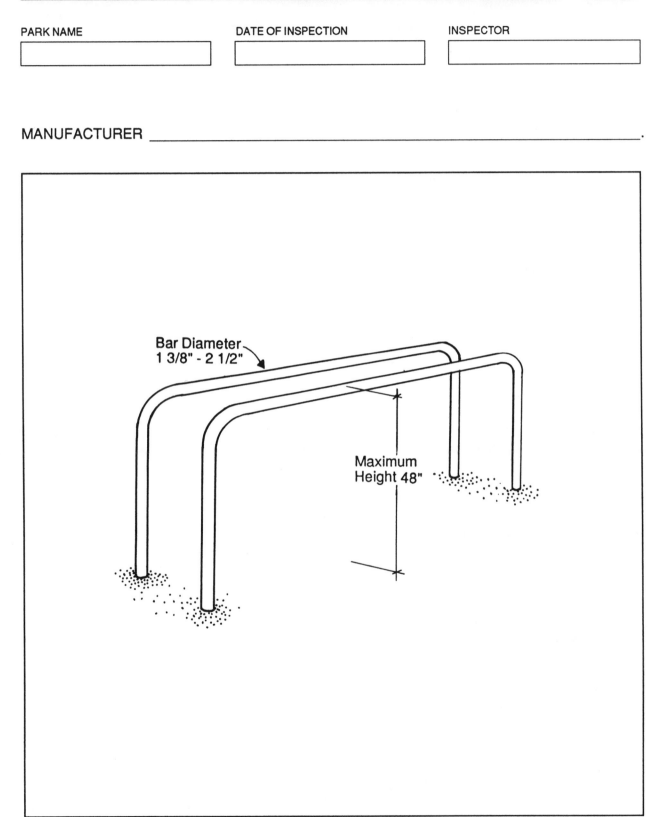

Bar Diameter
1 3/8" - 2 1/2"

Maximum
Height 48"

PARK NAME	DATE OF INSPECTION	INSPECTOR

If any of these items are NO, repair/remove the equipment immediately.

EQUIPMENT CONDITION/HEIGHT/FALL ZONE

1.	Is the equipment stable and without severe structural deterioration (e.g., at footings and joints)?	Yes	No	N/A
2.	Does the bar have an 8' obstruction-free fall zone?	Yes	No	N/A
3.	Is the parallel bar height 48" or less (36"-48" depending on size of average user)?	Yes	No	N/A

ENTRAPMENT

4.	Are all openings smaller than 3/8" or greater than 1" to prevent finger entrapment?	Yes	No	N/A
5.	Are openings smaller than 3" or larger than 9" to prevent head entrapment?	Yes	No	N/A
6.	Are angles greater than 55° to prevent head entrapment?	Yes	No	N/A

GENERAL CONSIDERATIONS

7.	Is the equipment complete without missing parts, free of vandalism which would impair safe use, and has no warping or bending of members.	Yes	No	N/A
8.	Is the equipment free from pinch or crush points?	Yes	No	N/A
9.	Is the equipment free from sharp points, corners, or edges?	Yes	No	N/A
10.	Is the equipment free from any protrusions (all nuts and bolts are recessed, fitted with tamper proof locks and the holes plugged)?	Yes	No	N/A
11.	Is the equipment free from suspended cables, wires, or ropes which would allow a rapidly moving child to impact his head or neck?	Yes	No	N/A

PARK NAME	DATE OF INSPECTION	INSPECTOR

12.	Is the pole diameter between 1-3/8" and 2-1/2"?	Yes No N/A
13.	Are the tops of concrete footings buried 12" below the ground level?	Yes No N/A
14.	Is the scale of the equipment appropriate to the size of the users?	Yes No N/A

HARDWARE

15.	Is all hardware present, securely attached, and without significant wear or evidence of deformation?	Yes No N/A
16.	Do fasteners and connecting devices require tools to loosen or remove them (i.e., no hex head bolts or nails are used)?	Yes No N/A

STRUCTURAL MATERIALS

The structure is made of _____.

For wood:

17.	Are load bearing members free from rot or insect damage?	Yes No N/A
18.	Are wood members free from checks more than 24" in length and/or 1/4" in width?	Yes No N/A
19.	If a wood preservative was used on the structure, list the preservative's name:_____.	
20.	Is the wood preservative safe for use in children's play areas?	Yes No N/A
21.	If a wood preservative was used, has a sealant been applied to treated areas every two years?	Yes No N/A

For Metal:

22.	If it is steel, is it galvanized or powder coated?	Yes No N/A

PARK NAME

DATE OF INSPECTION

INSPECTOR

23. If it is aluminum, is it powder coated or anodized?   Yes   No   N/A

24. Is the equipment free from rust on steel, corrosion on aluminum, or peeling paint?   Yes   No   N/A

For Plastic:

25. Are plastic parts unbroken and without chips or cracks, particularly at joints and connections?   Yes   No   N/A

For Paint:

26. If equipment is painted, was paint without lead used?   Yes   No   N/A

PARK NAME	DATE OF INSPECTION	INSPECTOR

BAR ACCESSIBILITY

27. Is the equipment accessible to individuals with the following disabilities (please check all that apply):　　Yes　　No　　N/A

- ❏ Wheelchair Users
- ❏ Developmentally Disabled
- ❏ Visually Impaired
- ❏ Cane/Crutch/Walker User
- ❏ Hearing Impaired
- ❏ Emotional/Behavioral Disability

28. Is there a way to make this piece usable by a great number of people with disabilities? (Please specify.)　　Yes　　No　　N/A

_____

_____

_____

_____

_____

_____

29. Can the equipment be adapted without creating a safety hazard for others?　　Yes　　No　　N/A

30. Can a person using a wheelchair, cane, crutches or other assistive device approach the equipment?　　Yes　　No　　N/A

31. Are clear sight lines provided from the equipment to adult supervision areas?　　Yes　　No　　N/A

32. Is the equipment easily understood?　　Yes　　No　　N/A

PARK NAME	DATE OF INSPECTION	INSPECTOR

Hazards are apparent from this inspection:

- ❑ Repair the problem,
- ❑ Submit a work order,
- ❑ Barricade or close the area, or
- ❑ Notify your supervisor.
- ❑ _____

PARALLEL BAR SAFETY RECOMMENDATIONS

- ❑ No Hazardous Conditions Found
- ❑ Removal/Repair Necessary (Prepare Work Order)

WORK ORDER

Item	Action	Date Completed	Time Spent	Cost ($)

PARALLEL BAR ACCESSIBILITY RECOMMENDATIONS

Item	Action	Date Completed	Time Spent	Cost ($)

PARK NAME

DATE OF INSPECTION

INSPECTOR

TYPE OF CLIMBER _____

MANUFACTURER _____

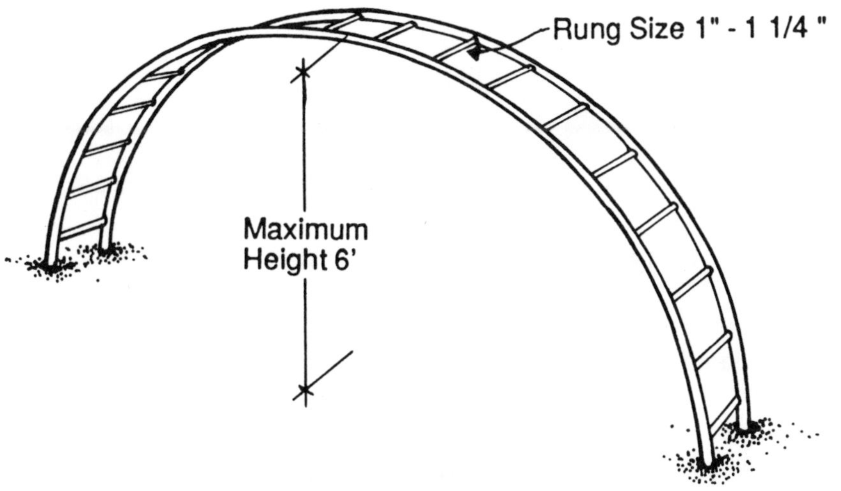

Rung Size 1" - 1 1/4 "

Maximum
Height 6'

PARK NAME	DATE OF INSPECTION	INSPECTOR

If any of these items are NO, repair/remove the equipment immediately.

EQUIPMENT CONDITION/HEIGHT/FALL ZONE

1. Is the equipment stable and without severe structural deterioration (e.g., at footings and joints)?   Yes   No   N/A

2. Does the climber have an 8' obstruction-free fall zone?   Yes   No   N/A

3. Is the climber height 6' or less?   Yes   No   N/A

ENTRAPMENT

4. Are all openings smaller than 3/8" or greater than 1" to prevent finger entrapment?   Yes   No   N/A

5. Are openings smaller than 3" or larger than 9" to prevent head entrapment?   Yes   No   N/A

6. Are angles greater than 55° to prevent head entrapment?   Yes   No   N/A

GENERAL CONSIDERATIONS

7. Is the equipment complete without missing parts, free of vandalism which would impair safe use, and has no warping or bending of members.   Yes   No   N/A

8. Is the equipment free from pinch or crush points?   Yes   No   N/A

9. Is the equipment free from sharp points, corners, or edges?   Yes   No   N/A

10. Is the equipment free from any protrusions (all nuts and bolts are recessed, fitted with tamper proof locks and the holes plugged)?   Yes   No   N/A

11. Is the equipment free from suspended cables, wires, or ropes which would allow a rapidly moving child to impact his head or neck?   Yes   No   N/A

PARK NAME	DATE OF INSPECTION	INSPECTOR

12. Are all platforms above 30" surrounded by non-climbable protective barriers at least 38" in height?　　Yes　　No　　N/A

13. Are the tops of concrete footings buried 12" below the ground level?　　Yes　　No　　N/A

14. Is the rung size between 1" and 1-1/4"?　　Yes　　No　　N/A

15. Is the scale of the equipment appropriate to the size of the users?　　Yes　　No　　N/A

HARDWARE

16. Is all hardware present, securely attached, and without significant wear or evidence of deformation?　　Yes　　No　　N/A

17. Do fasteners and connecting devices require tools to loosen or remove them (i.e., no hex head bolts or nails are used)?　　Yes　　No　　N/A

STRUCTURAL MATERIALS

The structure is made of _____.

For wood:

18. Are load bearing members free from rot or insect damage?　　Yes　　No　　N/A

19. Are wood members free from checks more than 24" in length and/or 1/4" in width?　　Yes　　No　　N/A

PARK NAME	DATE OF INSPECTION	INSPECTOR

20. If a wood preservative was used on the structure, list the preservative's name:_____.

21. Is the wood preservative safe for use in children's play areas?　　　Yes　　No　　N/A

22. If a wood preservative was used, has a sealant been applied to treated areas every two years?　　　Yes　　No　　N/A

For Metal:

23. If it is steel, is it galvanized or powder coated?　　　Yes　　No　　N/A

24. If it is aluminum, is it powder coated or anodized?　　　Yes　　No　　N/A

25. Is the equipment free from rust on steel, corrosion on aluminum, or peeling paint?　　　Yes　　No　　N/A

For Plastic:

26. Are plastic parts unbroken and without chips or cracks, particularly at joints and connections?　　　Yes　　No　　N/A

For Paint:

27. If equipment was painted, was paint without lead used?　　　Yes　　No　　N/A

PARK NAME

DATE OF INSPECTION

INSPECTOR

CLIMBER ACCESSIBILITY

28. Is the equipment accessible to individuals with the following disabilities (please check all that apply):   Yes   No   N/A

   ❑ Wheelchair Users   ❑ Cane/Crutch/Walker User
   ❑ Developmentally Disabled ❑ Hearing Impaired
   ❑ Visually Impaired   ❑ Emotional/Behavioral Disability

29. Is there a way to make this piece usable by a great number of people with disabilities? (Please specify.)   Yes   No   N/A

   _____

   _____

   _____

   _____

   _____

   _____

30. Can the equipment be adapted without creating a safety hazard for others?   Yes   No   N/A

31. Can a person using a wheelchair, cane, crutches or other assistive device approach the equipment?   Yes   No   N/A

32. Are clear sight lines provided from the top to the bottom of the equipment and from the equipment to adult supervision areas?   Yes   No   N/A

33. Is the equipment easily understood?   Yes   No   N/A

34. Does elevated equipment provide more than one means of exit of varying degrees of difficulty?   Yes   No   N/A

PARK NAME

DATE OF INSPECTION

INSPECTOR

Hazards are apparent from this inspection:

❏ Repair the problem,
❏ Submit a work order,
❏ Barricade or close the area, or
❏ Notify your supervisor.
❏ _____

CLIMBER SAFETY RECOMMENDATIONS

❏ No Hazardous Conditions Found
❏ Removal/Repair Necessary (Prepare Work Order)

WORK ORDER

Item	Action	Date Completed	Time Spent	Cost ($)

CLMBER ACCESSIBILITY RECOMMENDATIONS

Item	Action	Date Completed	Time Spent	Cost ($)

PARK NAME

DATE OF INSPECTION

INSPECTOR

TYPE OF CLIMBER _____

MANUFACTURER _____

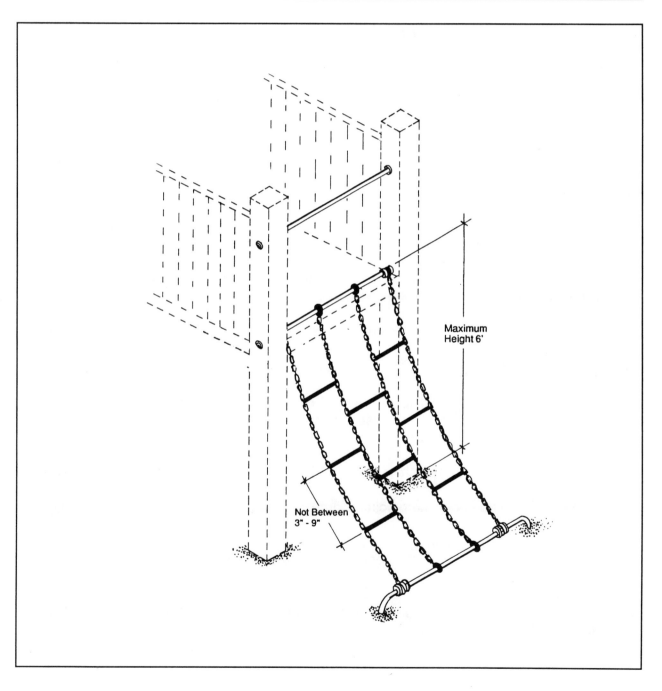

Maximum
Height 6'

Not Between
3" - 9"

PARK NAME	DATE OF INSPECTION	INSPECTOR

If any of these items are NO, repair/remove the equipment immediately.

EQUIPMENT CONDITION/HEIGHT/FALL ZONE

1. Is the equipment stable and without severe structural deterioration (e.g., at footings and joints)?   Yes   No   N/A

2. Does the equipment have an 8' obstruction-free fall zone?   Yes   No   N/A

3. Is the climber height 6' or less?   Yes   No   N/A

ENTRAPMENT

4. Are all openings smaller than 3/8" or greater than 1" to prevent finger entrapment?   Yes   No   N/A

5. Are openings smaller than 3" or larger than 9" to prevent head entrapment?   Yes   No   N/A

6. Are angles greater than 55° to prevent head entrapment?   Yes   No   N/A

GENERAL CONSIDERATIONS

7. Is the equipment complete without missing parts, free of vandalism which would impair safe use, and has no warping or bending of members.   Yes   No   N/A

8. Is the equipment free from pinch or crush points?   Yes   No   N/A

9. Is the equipment free from sharp points, corners, or edges?   Yes   No   N/A

10. Is the equipment free from any protrusions (all nuts and bolts are recessed, fitted with tamper proof locks and the holes plugged)?   Yes   No   N/A

11. Is the equipment free from suspended cables, wires, or ropes which would allow a rapidly moving child to impact his head or neck?   Yes   No   N/A

PARK NAME	DATE OF INSPECTION	INSPECTOR

12.	Are all platforms above 30" surrounded by non-climbable protective barriers at least 38" in height?	Yes	No	N/A
13.	Are the tops of concrete footings buried 12" below the ground level?	Yes	No	N/A
14.	Is the scale of the equipment appropriate to the size of the users?	Yes	No	N/A

CHAIN/ROPE/CABLE

15.	Is rope sound and in good repair?	Yes	No	N/A
16.	Is the chain in good condition without significant wear?	Yes	No	N/A
17.	Is the chain "proof coil" of 5/0 size with welded links?	Yes	No	N/A
18.	Is the cable in good condition without significant wear? (Cable splices and ends should be free of projecting wires.)	Yes	No	N/A

HARDWARE

19.	Is all hardware present, securely attached, and without significant wear or evidence of deformation?	Yes	No	N/A
20.	Do fasteners and connecting devices require tools to loosen or remove them (i.e., no hex head bolts or nails are used)?	Yes	No	N/A
21.	Are S-hooks and other connectors fully closed and secure?	Yes	No	N/A

PARK NAME	DATE OF INSPECTION	INSPECTOR

STRUCTURAL MATERIALS

The structure is made of _____ .

For Wood:

22. Are load bearing members free from rot or insect damage?   Yes   No   N/A

23. Are wood members free from checks more than 24" in length and/or 1/4" in width?   Yes   No   N/A

24. If a wood preservative was used on the structure, list the preservatives name:_____ .

25. Is the wood preservative safe for use in children's play areas?   Yes   No   N/A

26. If a wood preservative was used, has a sealant been applied to treated areas every two years?   Yes   No   N/A

For Metal:

27. If it is steel, is it galvanized or powder coated?   Yes   No   N/A

28. If it is aluminum, is it powder coated or anodized?   Yes   No   N/A

29. Is the equipment free from rust on steel, corrosion on aluminum, or peeling paint?   Yes   No   N/A

For Plastic:

30. Are plastic parts unbroken and without chips or cracks, particularly at joints and connections?   Yes   No   N/A

For Paint:

31. If equipment was painted, was paint without lead used?   Yes   No   N/A

PARK NAME

DATE OF INSPECTION

INSPECTOR

32. Is the equipment accessible to individuals with the following disabilities (please check all that apply):   Yes   No   N/A

    ❑ Wheelchair Users   ❑ Cane/Crutch/Walker User
    ❑ Developmentally Disabled   ❑ Hearing Impaired
    ❑ Visually Impaired   ❑ Emotional/Behavioral Disability

33. Is there a way to make this piece usable by a great number of people with disabilities? (Please specify.)   Yes   No   N/A

_____

_____

_____

_____

_____

34. Can the equipment be adapted without creating a safety hazard for others?   Yes   No   N/A

35. Can a person using a wheelchair, cane, crutches or other assistive device approach the equipment?   Yes   No   N/A

36. Are clear sight lines provided from the top to the bottom of the equipment and from the equipment to adult supervision areas?   Yes   No   N/A

37. Is the equipment easily understood?   Yes   No   N/A

38. Does elevated equipment provide more than one means of exit of varying degrees of difficulty?   Yes   No   N/A

CHAIN/ROPE CLIMBER RECOMMENDATIONS 7C

PARK NAME

DATE OF INSPECTION

INSPECTOR

Hazards are apparent from this inspection:

❑ Repair the problem,
❑ Submit a work order,
❑ Barricade or close the area, or
❑ Notify your supervisor.
❑ _____

CHAIN/ROPE CLIMBER SAFETY RECOMMENDATIONS

❑ No Hazardous Conditions Found
❑ Removal/Repair Necessary (Prepare Work Order)

WORK ORDER

Item	Action	Date Completed	Time Spent	Cost ($)

CHAIN/ROPE CLIMBER ACCESSIBILITY RECOMMENDATIONS

Item	Action	Date Completed	Time Spent	Cost ($)

PARK NAME

DATE OF INSPECTION

INSPECTOR

MANUFACTURER _____

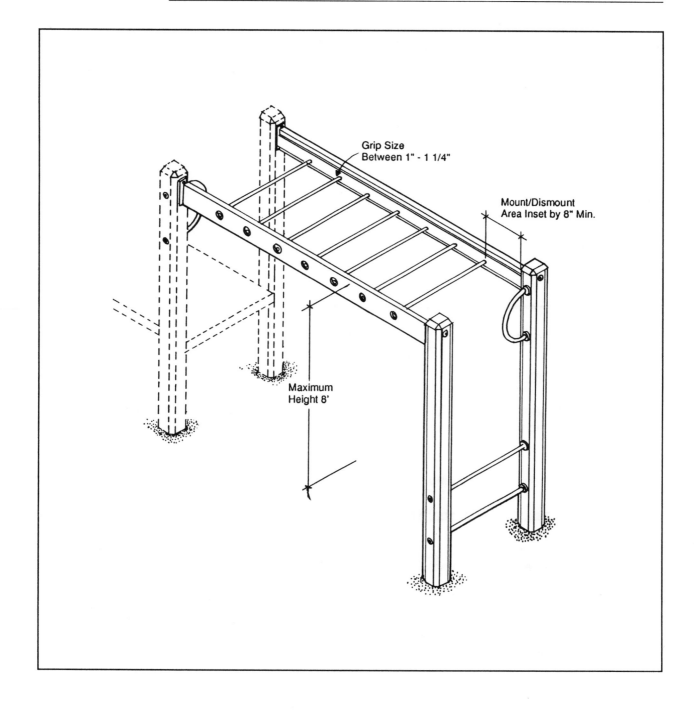

Grip Size
Between 1" - 1 1/4"

Mount/Dismount
Area Inset by 8" Min.

Maximum
Height 8'

PARK NAME	DATE OF INSPECTION	INSPECTOR

If any of these Items are NO, repair/remove the equipment Immediately.

EQUIPMENT CONDITION/HEIGHT/FALL ZONE

1. Is the equipment stable and without severe structural deterioration (e.g., at footings and joints)? Yes No N/A

2. Does the equipment have an 8' obstruction-free fall zone? Yes No N/A

3. Is the equipment height 8' or less? Yes No N/A

ENTRAPMENT

4. Are all openings smaller than 3/8" or greater than 1" to prevent finger entrapment? Yes No N/A

5. Are openings smaller than 3" or larger than 9" to prevent head entrapment? Yes No N/A

6. Are angles greater than 55° to prevent head entrapment? Yes No N/A

GENERAL CONSIDERATIONS

7. Is the equipment complete without missing parts, free of vandalism which would impair safe use, and has no warping or bending of members? Yes No N/A

8. Is the equipment free from pinch or crush points? Yes No N/A

9. Is the equipment free from sharp points, corners, or edges? Yes No N/A

10. Is the equipment free from any protrusions (all nuts and bolts are recessed, fitted with tamper proof locks and the holes plugged)? Yes No N/A

11. Is the equipment free from suspended cables, wires, or ropes which would allow a rapidly moving child to impact his head or neck? Yes No N/A

PARK NAME	DATE OF INSPECTION	INSPECTOR

12. Are all platforms above 30" surrounded by non-climbable protective barriers at least 38" in height?   Yes   No   N/A

13. Is the mount/dismount area inset by 8" or more from the rail or deck?   Yes   No   N/A

14. Is the grip size between 1" and 1-1/4"?   Yes   No   N/A

15. Are the rungs secure and without a tendency to rotate during use?   Yes   No   N/A

16. Are the tops of concrete footings buried 12" below the ground level?   Yes   No   N/A

17. Is the scale of the equipment appropriate to the size of the users?   Yes   No   N/A

HARDWARE

18. Is all hardware present, securely attached, and without significant wear or evidence of deformation?   Yes   No   N/A

19. Do fasteners and connecting devices require tools to loosen or remove them (i.e., no hex head bolts or nails are used)?   Yes   No   N/A

PARK NAME	DATE OF INSPECTION	INSPECTOR

STRUCTURAL MATERIALS

The structure is made of _____ .

For Wood:

20. Are load bearing members free from rot or insect damage?   Yes   No   N/A

21. Are wood members free from checks more than 24" in length and/or 1/4" in width?   Yes   No   N/A

22. If a wood preservative was used on the structure, list the preservatives name:_____ .

23. Is the wood preservative safe for use in children's play areas?   Yes   No   N/A

24. If a wood preservative was used, has a sealant been applied to treated areas every two years?   Yes   No   N/A

For Metal:

25. If it is steel, is it galvanized or powder coated?   Yes   No   N/A

26. If it is aluminum, is it powder coated or anodized?   Yes   No   N/A

27. Is the equipment free from rust on steel, corrosion on aluminum, or peeling paint?   Yes   No   N/A

For Paint:

28. If equipment was painted, was paint without lead used?   Yes   No   N/A

PARK NAME	DATE OF INSPECTION	INSPECTOR

HORIZONTAL LADDER ACCESSIBILITY

29. Is the equipment accessible to individuals with the following disabilities (please check all that apply):   Yes   No   N/A

   ❑ Wheelchair Users   ❑ Cane/Crutch/Walker Users

   ❑ Developmentally Disabled   ❑ Hearing Impaired

   ❑ Visually Impaired   ❑ Emotional/Behavioral Disability

30. Is there a way to make this piece usable by a greater number of people with disabilities? (Please specify.)   Yes   No   N/A

_____

_____

_____

_____

_____

_____

31. Can the equipment be adapted without creating a safety hazard for others?   Yes   No   N/A

32. Can a person using a wheelchair, cane, crutches or other assistive device approach the equipment?   Yes   No   N/A

33. Are clear sight lines provided from the top to the bottom of the equipment and from the equipment to adult supervision areas?   Yes   No   N/A

34. Is the equipment easily understood?   Yes   No   N/A

35. Does elevated equipment provide more than one means of exit of varying degrees of difficulty?   Yes   No   N/A

PARK NAME	DATE OF INSPECTION	INSPECTOR

Hazards are apparent from this inspection:

❏　Repair the problem,
❏　Submit a work order,
❏　Barricade or close the area, or
❏　Notify your supervisor.
❏　_____

HORIZONTAL LADDER SAFETY RECOMMENDATIONS

❏　No Hazardous Conditions Found
❏　Removal/Repair Necessary (Prepare Work Order)

WORK ORDER

Item	Action	Date Completed	Time Spent	Cost ($)

HORIZONTAL LADDER ACCESSIBILITY RECOMMENDATIONS

Item	Action	Date Completed	Time Spent	Cost ($)

PARK NAME

DATE OF INSPECTION

INSPECTOR

TYPE OF LADDER/STAIRWAY _____

MANUFACTURER _____

LADDER/STAIRWAY IS ATTACHED TO _____

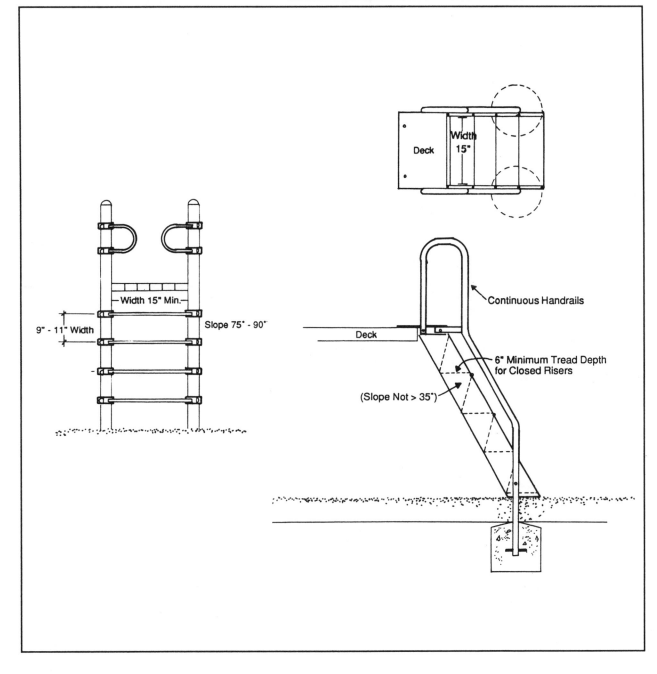

PARK NAME	DATE OF INSPECTION	INSPECTOR

For any equipment with a ladder or stairway, use the following questions to evaluate the rung/step safety.

If any of these items are answered NO, the equipment must be removed/repaired immediately.

1.	Do ladders with rungs have a slope of 75° – 90°?	Yes	No	N/A
2.	Do ladders with steps have a slope of 50° – 75°?	Yes	No	N/A
3.	Do stairways have a slope no greater than 35°?	Yes	No	N/A
4.	Are steps or rungs horizontal plus or minus 2°?	Yes	No	N/A
5.	Are steps or rungs at least 15" wide?	Yes	No	N/A
6.	Are rungs evenly spaced and between 9" and 11" apart (7" - 11" for closed risers)?(Measure between the top surfaces of two consecutive steps.)	Yes	No	N/A
7.	Is the step tread depth adequate? (3" or more for open risers; 6" or more for closed risers.)	Yes	No	N/A
8.	Do stairways and ladders with steps have continuous handrails on both sides designed to maintain the user in an upright position?(Handrails should not create a head entrapment.)	Yes	No	N/A
9.	Is the step or rung finish slip resistant?	Yes	No	N/A

Note:
35° = approx. 8½" vertical rise to a 12" horizontal run
50° = approx. 14½" vertical rise to a 12" horizontal run
75° = approx. 45" vertical rise to a 12" horizontal run

PARK NAME

DATE OF INSPECTION

INSPECTOR

Hazards are apparent from this inspection:

❑ Repair the problem,
❑ Submit a work order,
❑ Barricade or close the area, or
❑ Notify your supervisor.
❑ _____

LADDER/STAIRWAY SAFETY RECOMMENDATIONS

❑ No Hazardous Conditions Found
❑ Removal/Repair Necessary (Prepare Work Order)

WORK ORDER

Item	Action	Date Completed	Time Spent	Cost ($)

LADDER/STAIRWAY ACCESSIBILITY RECOMMENDATIONS

Item	Action	Date Completed	Time Spent	Cost ($)

PARK NAME

DATE OF INSPECTION

INSPECTOR

TYPE OF STRUCTURE (please describe) _____

_____

_____

MANUFACTURER _____

CHECK PLAY ELEMENTS INCLUDED:

- ❑ Balance Events
- ❑ Bannister Slide
- ❑ Climber
- ❑ Fire Pole
- ❑ Games
- ❑ Horizontal Ladder
- ❑ Moving Bridges
- ❑ Ring Trek

- ❑ Slide
- ❑ Spiral Slide
- ❑ Swings
- ❑ Tires
- ❑ Tire Swing
- ❑ Tot Swing
- ❑ Tunnel Slide
- ❑ Track Ride

- ❑ Tunnels
- ❑ Wheels
- ❑ Tic Tac Toe
- ❑ Play Panels
- ❑ Roofs
- ❑ Other _____
- ❑ Other _____
- ❑ Other _____

Maximum
Equipment
Height 8'

PARK NAME	DATE OF INSPECTION	INSPECTOR

To evaluate a linked structure, use this checklist section for each play element included in the structure, i.e. slide, tire swing, horizontal ladder, etc.

If any of these items is answered NO, repair/remove the equipment immediately.

EQUIPMENT CONDITION/HEIGHT/FALL ZONE

1. Is the equipment stable and without severe structural deterioration (e.g., at footings and joints)?   Yes   No   N/A

2. Does the equipment have an 8' obstruction-free fall zone?   Yes   No   N/A

3. If tire swings are included, are they separated from the fall zone of the main structure?   Yes   No   N/A

4. Is the maximum equipment height 8' or less? (6' for tire swing crossbeam.)   Yes   No   N/A

ENTRAPMENT

5. Are all openings smaller than 3/8" or greater than 1" to prevent finger entrapment?   Yes   No   N/A

6. Are openings smaller than 3" or larger than 9" to prevent head entrapment?   Yes   No   N/A

7. Are angles greater than 55° to prevent head entrapment?   Yes   No   N/A

GENERAL CONSIDERATIONS

8. Is the equipment complete without missing parts, free of vandalism which would impair safe use, and has no warping or bending of members.   Yes   No   N/A

9. Is the equipment free from pinch or crush points?   Yes   No   N/A

10. Is the equipment free from sharp points, corners, or edges?   Yes   No   N/A

PARK NAME	DATE OF INSPECTION	INSPECTOR

11.	Is the equipment free from any protrusions (all nuts and bolts are recessed, fitted with tamper proof locks and the holes plugged)?	Yes No N/A
12.	Is the equipment free from suspended cables, wires, or ropes which would allow a rapidly moving child to impact his head or neck?	Yes No N/A
13.	Are all platforms above 30" surrounded by non-climbable protective barriers at least 38" in height?	Yes No N/A
14.	Are the tops of concrete footings buried 12" below the ground level?	Yes No N/A
15.	Is the scale of the equipment appropriate to the size of the users?	Yes No N/A

CHAIN/ROPE/CABLE

16.	Is rope sound and in good repair?	Yes No N/A
17.	Is the chain in good condition without significant wear?	Yes No N/A
18.	Is the chain "proof coil" of 5/0 size with welded links?	Yes No N/A
19.	Is the cable in good condition without significant wear? (Cable splices and ends should free of projecting wires.)	Yes No N/A

HARDWARE

20.	Is all hardware present, securely attached, and without significant wear or evidence of deformation?	Yes No N/A
21.	Do fasteners and connecting devices require tools to loosen or remove them (i.e., no hex head bolts or nails are used)?	Yes No N/A
22.	Are S-hooks and other connectors fully closed and secure?	Yes No N/A

PARK NAME

DATE OF INSPECTION

INSPECTOR

STRUCTURAL MATERIALS

The structure is made of _____.

For Wood:

23. Are load bearing members free from rot or insect damage?   Yes   No   N/A

24. Are wood members free from checks more than 24" in length and/or 1/4" in width?   Yes   No   N/A

25. If a wood preservative was used on the structure, list the preservatives name:_____.

26. Is the wood preservative safe for use in children's play areas?   Yes   No   N/A

27. If a wood preservative was used, has a sealant been applied to treated areas every two years?   Yes   No   N/A

For Metal:

28. If it is steel, is it galvanized or powder coated?   Yes   No   N/A

29. If it is aluminum, is it powder coated or anodized?   Yes   No   N/A

30. Is the equipment free from rust on steel, corrosion on aluminum, or peeling paint?   Yes   No   N/A

For Plastic:

31. Are plastic parts unbroken and without chips or cracks, particularly at joints and connections?   Yes   No   N/A

For Paint:

32. If equipment was painted, was paint without lead used?   Yes   No   N/A

PARK NAME	DATE OF INSPECTION	INSPECTOR

LINKED STRUCTURE ACCESSIBILITY

33. Is the equipment accessible to individuals with the following disabilities (please check all that apply):   Yes   No   N/A

❑ Wheelchair Users   ❑ Cane/Crutch/Walker Users

❑ Developmentally Disabled   ❑ Hearing Impaired

❑ Visually Impaired   ❑ Emotional/Behavioral Disability

34. Is there a way to make this piece usable by a great number of people with disabilities? (Please specify.)   Yes   No   N/A

_____

_____

_____

_____

_____

_____

35. Can the equipment be adapted without creating a safety hazard for others?   Yes   No   N/A

36. Can a person using a wheelchair, cane, crutches or other assistive device approach the equipment?   Yes   No   N/A

37. Are clear sight lines provided from the top to the bottom of the equipment and from the equipment to adult supervision areas?   Yes   No   N/A

38. Is the equipment easily understood?   Yes   No   N/A

39. Does elevated equipment provide more than one means of exit of varying degrees of difficulty?   Yes   No   N/A

LINKED STRUCTURE RECOMMENDATIONS | 10C

PARK NAME

DATE OF INSPECTION

INSPECTOR

Hazards are apparent from this inspection:

❏ Repair the problem,
❏ Submit a work order,
❏ Barricade or close the area, or
❏ Notify your supervisor.
❏ _____

LINKED STRUCTURE SAFETY RECOMMENDATIONS

❏ No Hazardous Conditions Found
❏ Removal/Repair Necessary (Prepare Work Order)

WORK ORDER

Item	Action	Date Completed	Time Spent	Cost ($)

LINKED STRUCTURE ACCESSIBILITY RECOMMENDATIONS

Item	Action	Date Completed	Time Spent	Cost ($)

PARK NAME

DATE OF INSPECTION

INSPECTOR

TYPE OF MERRY-GO-ROUND / WHIRL _____.

MANUFACTURER _____.

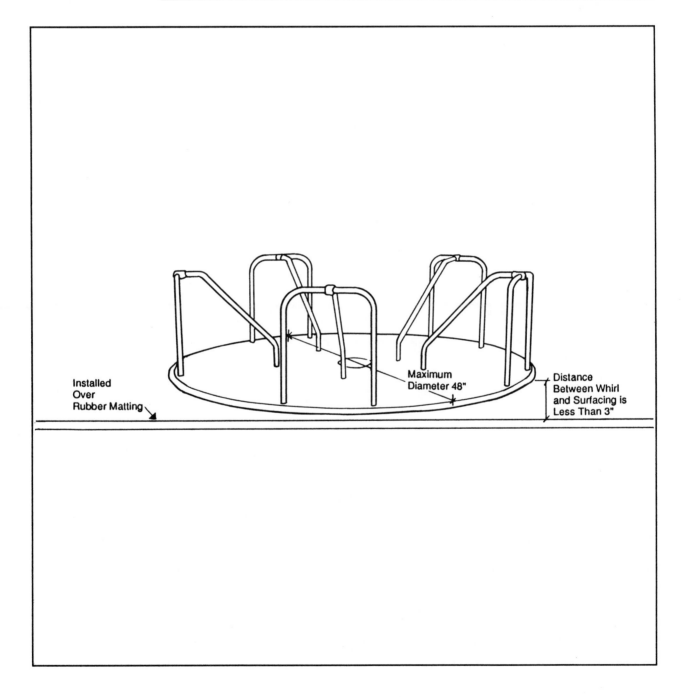

Installed Over Rubber Matting

Maximum Diameter 48"

Distance Between Whirl and Surfacing is Less Than 3"

PARK NAME

DATE OF INSPECTION

INSPECTOR

If any of these items is answered NO, repair/remove the equipment immediately.

EQUIPMENT CONDITION/HEIGHT/FALL ZONE

1. Is the equipment stable and without severe structural deterioration (e.g., at footings and joints)?   Yes   No   N/A

2. Is the whirl platform level and remains level when unevenly laden?   Yes   No   N/A

3. Does the equipment have an 8' obstruction-free fall zone?   Yes   No   N/A

4. Is the spinning equipment installed over rubber matting?   Yes   No   N/A

5. Is the distance between the whirl and surfacing less than 3"?   Yes   No   N/A

6. Is the equipment free from components which extend beyond the perimeter of the base?   Yes   No   N/A

ENTRAPMENT

7. Are all openings smaller than 3/8" or greater than 1" to prevent finger entrapment?   Yes   No   N/A

8. Are openings smaller than 3" or larger than 9" to prevent head entrapment?   Yes   No   N/A

9. Are angles greater than 55° to prevent head entrapment?   Yes   No   N/A

10. Is the spinning equipment free from open framework and gaps in the central support post and the whirl?   Yes   No   N/A

GENERAL CONSIDERATIONS

11. Is the equipment complete without missing parts, free of vandalism which would impair safe use, and has no warping or bending of members.   Yes   No   N/A

12. Is the equipment free from pinch or crush points?   Yes   No   N/A

PARK NAME	DATE OF INSPECTION	INSPECTOR

13. Is the equipment free from sharp points, corners, or edges? Yes No N/A

14. Is the equipment free from any protrusions (all nuts and bolts are recessed, fitted with tamper proof locks and the holes plugged)? Yes No N/A

15. Is the difference between the minimum and maximum radii of a non-circular base 2" or less? Yes No N/A

16. Is the diameter of the whirl base 48" or less? Yes No N/A

HARDWARE

17. Is all hardware present, securely attached, and without significant wear or evidence of deformation? Yes No N/A

18. Do fasteners and connecting devices require tools to loosen or remove them (i.e., no hex head bolts or nails are used)? Yes No N/A

STRUCTURAL MATERIALS

The structure is made of _____.

For Wood:

19. Are load bearing members free from rot or insect damage? Yes No N/A

20. Are wood members free from checks more than 24" in length and/or 1/4" in width? Yes No N/A

21. If a wood preservative was used on the structure, list the preservative's name:_____.

22. Is the wood preservative safe for use in children's play areas? Yes No N/A

23. If a wood preservative was used, has a sealant been applied to treated areas every two years? Yes No N/A

PARK NAME

DATE OF INSPECTION

INSPECTOR

For Metal:

24. If it is steel, is it galvanized or powder coated?   Yes   No   N/A

25. If it is aluminum, is it powder coated or anodized?   Yes   No   N/A

26. Is the equipment free from rust on steel, corrosion on aluminum, or peeling paint?   Yes   No   N/A

For Plastic:

Not recommended material for whirls in public play settings.

For Paint:

27. If equipment was painted, was paint without lead used?   Yes   No   N/A

PARK NAME

DATE OF INSPECTION

INSPECTOR

MERRY-GO ROUND / WHIRL ACCESSIBILITY

28. Is the equipment accessible to individuals with the following disabilities (please check all that apply):   Yes   No   N/A

   ❏ Wheelchair Users   ❏ Cane/Crutch/Walker Users
   ❏ Developmentally Disabled   ❏ Hearing Impaired
   ❏ Visually Impaired   ❏ Emotional/Behavioral Disability

29. Is there a way to make this piece usable by a greater number of people with disabilities? (Please specify.)   Yes   No   N/A

   _____

   _____

   _____

   _____

   _____

30. Can the equipment be adapted without creating a safety hazard for others?   Yes   No   N/A

31. Can a person using a wheelchair, cane, crutches or other assistive device approach the equipment?   Yes   No   N/A

32. Are clear sight lines provided to adult supervision areas?   Yes   No   N/A

33. Is the equipment easily understood?   Yes   No   N/A

MERRY-GO-ROUND RECOMMENDATIONS   11C

PARK NAME

DATE OF INSPECTION

INSPECTOR

Hazards are apparent from this inspection:

❑ Repair the problem,
❑ Submit a work order,
❑ Barricade or close the area, or
❑ Notify your supervisor.
❑ _____

MERRY-GO-ROUND/WHIRL SAFETY RECOMMENDATIONS

❑ No Hazardous Conditions Found
❑ Removal/Repair Necessary (Prepare Work Order)

WORK ORDER

Item	Action	Date Completed	Time Spent	Cost ($)

MERRY-GO-ROUND/WHIRL ACCESSIBILITY RECOMMENDATIONS

Item	Action	Date Completed	Time Spent	Cost ($)

PARK NAME

DATE OF INSPECTION

INSPECTOR

TYPE OF MOVING BRIDGE_____

MANUFACTURER _____

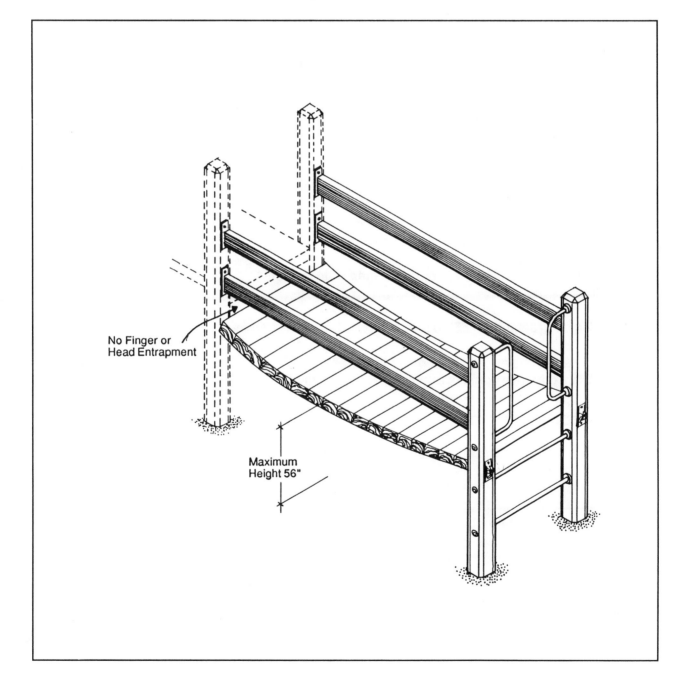

No Finger or
Head Entrapment

Maximum
Height 56"

PARK NAME	DATE OF INSPECTION	INSPECTOR

If any of these Items Is answered NO, repair/remove the equipment Immediately.

EQUIPMENT CONDITION/HEIGHT/FALL ZONE

1. Is the equipment stable and without severe structural deterioration (e.g., at footings and joints)?   Yes   No   N/A

2. Does the bridge have an 8' obstruction-free fall zone?   Yes   No   N/A

3. Is the height 56" or less to the bridge surface?   Yes   No   N/A

ENTRAPMENT

4. Are all openings smaller than 3/8" or greater than 1" to prevent finger entrapment?   Yes   No   N/A

5. Are openings smaller than 3" or larger than 9" to prevent head entrapment?   Yes   No   N/A

6. Are angles greater than 55° to prevent head entrapment?   Yes   No   N/A

7. Are cables or chains tight enough so that there is no possibility that they could overlap and entrap a child?   Yes   No   N/A

GENERAL CONSIDERATIONS

8. Is the equipment complete without missing parts, free of vandalism which would impair safe use, and has no warping or bending of members.   Yes   No   N/A

9. Is the equipment free from pinch or crush points?   Yes   No   N/A

10. Is the equipment free from sharp points, corners, or edges?   Yes   No   N/A

11. Is the equipment free from any protrusions (all nuts and bolts are recessed, fitted with tamper proof locks and the holes plugged)?   Yes   No   N/A

PARK NAME	DATE OF INSPECTION	INSPECTOR

12. Is the equipment free from suspended cables, wires, or ropes which would allow a rapidly moving child to impact his head or neck?　　　Yes　No　N/A

13. Are all platforms above 30" surrounded by non-climbable protective barriers at least 38" in height?　　　Yes　No　N/A

14. Are all connection points sound and without significant wear?　　　Yes　No　N/A

15. Are planks secure, splinter free and free of protruding hardware?　　　Yes　No　N/A

16. Are the tops of concrete footings buried 12" below the ground level?　　　Yes　No　N/A

17. Is the scale of the equipment appropriate to the size of the users?　　　Yes　No　N/A

CHAIN/CABLE/ROPE

18. Is rope sound and in good repair?　　　Yes　No　N/A

19. Is the chain in good condition without significant wear?　　　Yes　No　N/A

20. Is the chain "proof coil" of 5/0 size with welded links?　　　Yes　No　N/A

21. Is the cable in good condition without significant wear? Are cable splices and ends free of projecting wires?　　　Yes　No　N/A

HARDWARE

22. Is all hardware present, securely attached, and without significant wear or evidence of deformation?　　　Yes　No　N/A

23. Do fasteners and connecting devices require tools to loosen or remove them (i.e., no hex head bolts or nails are used)?　　　Yes　No　N/A

24. Are bearings in good condition and well lubricated?　　　Yes　No　N/A

25. Are S-hooks and other connectors fully closed and secure?　　　Yes　No　N/A

PARK NAME	DATE OF INSPECTION	INSPECTOR

STRUCTURAL MATERIALS

The structure is made of _____ .

For Wood:

26. Are load bearing members free from rot or insect damage?   Yes   No   N/A

27. Are wood members free from checks more than 24" in length and/or 1/4" in width?   Yes   No   N/A

28. If a wood preservative was used on the structure, list the preservatives name:_____ .

29. Is the wood preservative safe for use in children's play areas?   Yes   No   N/A

30. If a wood preservative was used, has a sealant been applied to treated areas every two years?   Yes   No   N/A

For Metal:

31. If it is steel, is it galvanized or powder coated?   Yes   No   N/A

32. If it is aluminum, is it powder coated or anodized?   Yes   No   N/A

33. Is the equipment free from rust on steel, corrosion on aluminum, or peeling paint?   Yes   No   N/A

For Plastic:

34. Are plastic parts unbroken and without chips or cracks, particularly at joints and connections?   Yes   No   N/A

For Paint:

35. If equipment was painted, was paint without lead used?   Yes   No   N/A

PARK NAME	DATE OF INSPECTION	INSPECTOR

MOVING BRIDGE ACCESSIBILITY

36. Is the equipment accessible to individuals with the following disabilities (please check all that apply):   Yes   No   N/A

     ❑ Wheelchair Users   ❑ Cane/Crutch/Walker Users

     ❑ Developmentally Disabled   ❑ Hearing Impaired

     ❑ Visually Impaired   ❑ Emotional/Behavioral Disability

37. Is there a way to make this piece usable by a greater number of people with disabilities? (Please specify.)   Yes   No   N/A

_____

_____

_____

_____

_____

_____

38. Can the equipment be adapted without creating a safety hazard for others?   Yes   No   N/A

39. Can a person using a wheelchair, cane, crutches or other assistive device approach the equipment?   Yes   No   N/A

40. Are clear sight lines provided from the top to the bottom of the equipment and from the equipment to adult supervision areas?   Yes   No   N/A

41. Is the equipment easily understood?   Yes   No   N/A

42. Does elevated equipment provide more than one means of exit of varying degrees of difficulty?   Yes   No   N/A

MOVING BRIDGE RECOMMENDATIONS

PARK NAME	DATE OF INSPECTION	INSPECTOR

Hazards are apparent from this inspection:

☐ Repair the problem,
☐ Submit a work order,
☐ Barricade or close the area, or
☐ Notify your supervisor.
☐ _____

MOVING BRIDGE SAFETY RECOMMENDATIONS

☐ No Hazardous Conditions Found
☐ Removal/Repair Necessary (Prepare Work Order)

WORK ORDER

Item	Action	Date Completed	Time Spent	Cost ($)

MOVING BRIDGE ACCESSIBILITY RECOMMENDATIONS

Item	Action	Date Completed	Time Spent	Cost ($)

PARK NAME

DATE OF INSPECTION

INSPECTOR

TYPE OF PLAYHOUSE _____

MANUFACTURER _____

Minimum
Interior
Height 4'

Maximum
Exterior
Height 6'

PLAYHOUSE SAFETY   13A

PARK NAME	DATE OF INSPECTION	INSPECTOR

If any of these Items Is answered NO, repair/remove the equipment Immediately.

EQUIPMENT CONDITION/HEIGHT/FALL ZONE

1. Is the equipment stable and without severe structural deterioration (e.g., at footings and joints)? Yes   No   N/A

2. If the playhouse is climbable, does it have an 8' obstruction-free fall zone? Yes   No   N/A

3. Is the structure high enough that an average child (4 feet) can stand safely inside without hitting his head? Yes   No   N/A

4. Is the structure's exterior height a maximum of 6'? Yes   No   N/A

ENTRAPMENT

5. Are all openings smaller than 3/8" or greater than 1" to prevent finger entrapment? Yes   No   N/A

6. Are openings smaller than 3" or larger than 9" to prevent head entrapment? Yes   No   N/A

7. Are angles greater than 55° to prevent head entrapment? Yes   No   N/A

GENERAL CONSIDERATIONS

8. Is the equipment complete without missing parts, free of vandalism which would impair safe use, and has no warping or bending of members. Yes   No   N/A

9. Is the equipment free from pinch or crush points? Yes   No   N/A

10. Is the equipment free from sharp points, corners, or edges? Yes   No   N/A

11. Is the playhouse free from any protrusions (all nuts and bolts are recessed, fitted with tamper proof locks and the holes plugged)? Yes   No   N/A

PARK NAME

DATE OF INSPECTION

INSPECTOR

12. Is the playhouse free from suspended cables, wires, or ropes which would allow a rapidly moving child to impact his head or neck?   Yes   No   N/A

13. Are the tops of concrete footings buried 12" below the ground level?   Yes   No   N/A

14. Are all platforms above 30" surrounded by non-climbable protective barriers at least 38" in height?   Yes   No   N/A

15. Is there a minimum of two exits?   Yes   No   N/A

16. Are the windows low enough and large enough to climb in and out?   Yes   No   N/A

17. If there is a roof, is it waterproof?   Yes   No   N/A

18. Is there an overhang on the roof?   Yes   No   N/A

19. Is the roof strong enough to be climbed upon?   Yes   No   N/A

20. Is there visibility from the outside into the structure?   Yes   No   N/A

21. Is the scale of the equipment appropriate to the size of the users?   Yes   No   N/A

HARDWARE

22. Is all hardware present, securely attached, and without significant wear or evidence of deformation?   Yes   No   N/A

23. Do fasteners and connecting devices require tools to loosen or remove them (i.e., no hex head bolts or nails are used)?   Yes   No   N/A

PARK NAME	DATE OF INSPECTION	INSPECTOR

STRUCTURAL MATERIALS

The structure is made of _____ .

For Wood:

24. Are load bearing members free from rot or insect damage?   Yes   No   N/A

25. Are wood members free from checks more than 24" in length and/or 1/4" in width?   Yes   No   N/A

26. If a wood preservative was used on the structure, list the preservatives name:_____.

27. Is the wood preservative safe for use in children's play areas?   Yes   No   N/A

28. If a wood preservative was used, has a sealant been applied to treated areas every two years?   Yes   No   N/A

For Metal:

29. If it is steel, is it galvanized or powder coated?   Yes   No   N/A

30. If it is aluminum, is it powder coated or anodized?   Yes   No   N/A

31. Is the equipment free from rust on steel, corrosion on aluminum, or peeling paint?   Yes   No   N/A

For Plastic:

32. Are plastic parts unbroken and without chips or cracks, particularly at joints and connections?   Yes   No   N/A

For Paint:

33. If equipment was painted, was paint without lead used?   Yes   No   N/A

PARK NAME	DATE OF INSPECTION	INSPECTOR

PLAYHOUSE ACCESSIBILITY

34. Is the equipment accessible to individuals with the   Yes   No   N/A
following disabilities (please check all that apply):

   ❑ Wheelchair Users   ❑ Cane/Crutch/Walker Users
   ❑ Developmentally Disabled   ❑ Hearing Impaired
   ❑ Visually Impaired   ❑ Emotional/Behavioral Disability

35. Is there a way to make this piece usable by a greater   Yes   No   N/A
number of people with disabilities? (Please specify.)

_____

_____

_____

_____

_____

36. Can the equipment be adapted without creating a safety   Yes   No   N/A
hazard for others?

37. Can a person using a wheelchair, cane, crutches or other   Yes   No   N/A
assistive device approach the equipment?

38. Can a child in a wheelchair get through the doorway?   Yes   No   N/A

39. Are clear sight lines provided from the top to the bottom of   Yes   No   N/A
the equipment and from the equipment to adult supervision
areas?

40. Is the equipment easily understood?   Yes   No   N/A

PLAYHOUSE RECOMMENDATIONS

PARK NAME	DATE OF INSPECTION	INSPECTOR

Hazards are apparent from this inspection:

- ❑ Repair the problem,
- ❑ Submit a work order,
- ❑ Barricade or close the area, or
- ❑ Notify your supervisor.
- ❑ _____

PLAYHOUSE SAFETY RECOMMENDATIONS

- ❑ No Hazardous Conditions Found
- ❑ Removal/Repair Necessary (Prepare Work Order)

WORK ORDER

Item	Action	Date Completed	Time Spent	Cost ($)

PLAYHOUSE ACCESSIBILITY RECOMMENDATIONS

Item	Action	Date Completed	Time Spent	Cost ($)

PARK NAME

DATE OF INSPECTION

INSPECTOR

TYPE OF EQUIPMENT_____

MANUFACTURER _____

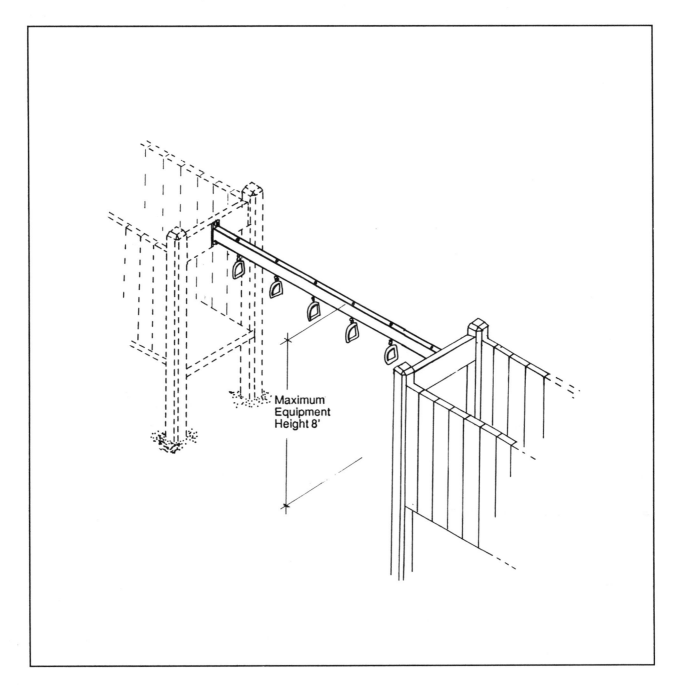

Maximum
Equipment
Height 8'

PARK NAME	DATE OF INSPECTION	INSPECTOR

If any of these items is answered NO, repair/remove the equipment immediately.

EQUIPMENT CONDITION/HEIGHT/FALL ZONE

1. Is the equipment stable and without severe structural deterioration (e.g., at footings and joints)? Yes No N/A

2. Does the equipment have an 8' obstruction-free fall zone? Yes No N/A

3. Is the equipment height 8' or under? Yes No N/A

ENTRAPMENT

4. Are all openings smaller than 3/8" or greater than 1" to prevent finger entrapment? Yes No N/A

5. Are openings smaller than 3" or larger than 9" to prevent head entrapment? Yes No N/A

6. Are angles greater than 55° to prevent head entrapment? Yes No N/A

GENERAL CONSIDERATIONS

7. Is the equipment complete without missing parts, free of vandalism which would impair safe use, and has no warping or bending of members. Yes No N/A

8. Is the equipment free from pinch or crush points? Yes No N/A

9. Is the equipment free from sharp points, corners, or edges? Yes No N/A

10. Is the equipment free from any protrusions (all nuts and bolts are recessed, fitted with tamper proof locks and the holes plugged)? Yes No N/A

11. Is the equipment free from suspended cables, wires, or ropes which would allow a rapidly moving child to impact his head or neck? Yes No N/A

PARK NAME	DATE OF INSPECTION	INSPECTOR

12. Are the tops of concrete footings buried 12" below the ground level?   Yes   No   N/A

13. Is the scale of the equipment appropriate to the size of the users?   Yes   No   N/A

14. Can the ring assembly withstand a weight of 1200 lbs. when tested according to the NBS method? (Apply the force at 120° gradually until it reaches 1200 lbs., then hold it for 5 minutes. For information on a testing device contact Paul Hogan, Playground Clearinghouse, 26 Buckwalter Rd., Phoenixville, PA 19460, 215-935-1549.)   Yes   No   N/A

15. Are rails and grips between 1" and 1-1/4" in diameter?   Yes   No   N/A

CHAIN AND CABLE

16. Is the chain length 12" or less?   Yes   No   N/A

17. Is the chain in good condition without significant wear?   Yes   No   N/A

18. Is the chain "proof coil" of 5/0 size with welded links?   Yes   No   N/A

19. Is the cable in good condition without significant wear? Are cable splices and ends free of projecting wires?   Yes   No   N/A

HARDWARE

20. Is all hardware present, securely attached, and without significant wear or evidence of deformation?   Yes   No   N/A

21. Do fasteners and connecting devices require tools to loosen or remove them (i.e., no hex head bolts or nails are used)?   Yes   No   N/A

PARK NAME	DATE OF INSPECTION	INSPECTOR

22. Are bearings in good condition and well lubricated?   Yes   No   N/A

23. Are S-hooks and other connectors fully closed and secure?   Yes   No   N/A

STRUCTURAL MATERIALS

The structure is made of _____.

For Wood:

24. Are load bearing members free from rot or insect damage?   Yes   No   N/A

25. Are wood members free from checks more than 24" in length and/or 1/4" in width?   Yes   No   N/A

26. If a wood preservative was used on the structure, list the preservative's name:_____.

27. Is the wood preservative safe for use in children's play areas?   Yes   No   N/A

28. If a wood preservative was used, has a sealant been applied to treated areas every two years?   Yes   No   N/A

For Metal:

29. If it is steel, is it galvanized or powder coated?   Yes   No   N/A

30. If it is aluminum, is it powder coated or anodized?   Yes   No   N/A

31. Is the equipment free from rust on steel, corrosion on aluminum, or peeling paint?   Yes   No   N/A

For Paint

32. If equipment was painted, was paint without lead used?   Yes   No   N/A

PARK NAME	DATE OF INSPECTION	INSPECTOR

RING TREK/TRACK RIDE ACCESSIBILITY

33. Is the equipment accessible to individuals with the following disabilities (please check all that apply):　　　Yes　　No　　N/A

❑ Wheelchair Users　　　　❑ Cane/Crutch/Walker Users
❑ Developmentally Disabled　　❑ Hearing Impaired
❑ Visually Impaired　　　　❑ Emotional/Behavioral Disability

34. Is there a way to make this piece usable by a greater number of people with disabilities? (Please specify.)　　Yes　　No　　N/A

_____

_____

_____

_____

_____

_____

35. Can the equipment be adapted without creating a safety hazard for others?　　Yes　　No　　N/A

36. Can a person using a wheelchair, cane, crutches or other assistive device approach the equipment?　　Yes　　No　　N/A

37. Are clear sight lines provided from the top to the bottom of the equipment and from the equipment to adult supervision areas?　　Yes　　No　　N/A

38. Is the equipment easily understood?　　Yes　　No　　N/A

39. Does elevated equipment provide more than one means of exit of varying degrees of difficulty?　　Yes　　No　　N/A

PARK NAME

DATE OF INSPECTION

INSPECTOR

Hazards are apparent from this inspection:

❑ Repair the problem,
❑ Submit a work order,
❑ Barricade or close the area, or
❑ Notify your supervisor.
❑ _____

RING TREK/TRACK RIDE SAFETY RECOMMENDATIONS

❑ No Hazardous Conditions Found
❑ Removal/Repair Necessary (Prepare Work Order)

WORK ORDER

Item	Action	Date Completed	Time Spent	Cost ($)

RING TREK/TRACK RIDE ACCESSIBILITY RECOMMENDATIONS

Item	Action	Date Completed	Time Spent	Cost ($)

PARK NAME

DATE OF INSPECTION

INSPECTOR

TYPE OF STRUCTURE (please describe) _____

_____

_____

MANUFACTURER _____

CHECK PLAY ELEMENTS INCLUDED:

- ❏ Balance Events
- ❏ Bannister Slide
- ❏ Climber
- ❏ Fire Pole
- ❏ Games
- ❏ Horizontal Ladder
- ❏ Moving Bridges
- ❏ Ring Trek

- ❏ Slide
- ❏ Spiral Slide
- ❏ Swings
- ❏ Tires
- ❏ Tire Swing
- ❏ Tot Swing
- ❏ Tunnel Slide
- ❏ Track Ride

- ❏ Tunnels
- ❏ Wheels
- ❏ Tic Tac Toe
- ❏ Play Panels
- ❏ Roofs
- ❏ Other _____
- ❏ Other _____
- ❏ Other _____

Use this space to draw a sketch of the equipment.

PARK NAME

DATE OF INSPECTION

INSPECTOR

To evaluate site built equipment, use this checklist section and/or any combination of sections which best describes the structure, e.g. climber, tunnel, etc.

If any of these items is answered NO, repair/remove the equipment immediately.

EQUIPMENT CONDITION/HEIGHT/FALL ZONE

1.	Is the equipment stable and without severe structural deterioration (e.g., at footings and joints)?	Yes	No	N/A
2.	Does the equipment have an 8' obstruction-free fall zone?	Yes	No	N/A
3.	Is the height 6' or less?	Yes	No	N/A

ENTRAPMENT

4.	Are all openings smaller than 3/8" or greater than 1" to prevent finger entrapment?	Yes	No	N/A
5.	Are openings smaller than 3" or larger than 9" to prevent head entrapment?	Yes	No	N/A
6.	Are angles greater than 55° to prevent head entrapment?	Yes	No	N/A

GENERAL CONSIDERATIONS

7.	Is the equipment complete without missing parts, free of vandalism which would impair safe use, and has no warping or bending of members.	Yes	No	N/A
8.	Is the equipment free from pinch or crush points?	Yes	No	N/A
9.	Is the equipment free from sharp points, corners, or edges?	Yes	No	N/A
10.	Is the equipment free from any protrusions (all nuts and bolts are recessed, fitted with tamper proof locks and the holes plugged)?	Yes	No	N/A

PARK NAME

DATE OF INSPECTION

INSPECTOR

11. Is the equipment free from suspended cables, wires, or ropes which would allow a rapidly moving child to impact his head or neck?   Yes   No   N/A

12. Are all platforms above 30" surrounded by non-climbable protective barriers at least 38" in height?   Yes   No   N/A

13. Are the tops of concrete footings buried 12" below the ground level?   Yes   No   N/A

14. Is the scale of the equipment appropriate to the size of the users?   Yes   No   N/A

CHAIN/CABLE/ROPE

15. Is rope sound and in good repair?   Yes   No   N/A

16. Is the chain in good condition without significant wear?   Yes   No   N/A

17. Is the chain "proof coil" of 5/0 size with welded links?   Yes   No   N/A

18. Is the cable in good condition without significant wear? (Cable splices and ends should be free of projecting wires.)   Yes   No   N/A

HARDWARE

19. Is all hardware present, securely attached, and without significant wear or evidence of deformation?   Yes   No   N/A

20. Do fasteners and connecting devices require tools to loosen or remove them (i.e., no hex head bolts or nails are used)?   Yes   No   N/A

21. Are bearings in good condition and well lubricated?   Yes   No   N/A

22. Are S-hooks and other connectors fully closed and secure?   Yes   No   N/A

PARK NAME

DATE OF INSPECTION

INSPECTOR

STRUCTURAL MATERIALS

The structure is made of _____ .

For Wood:

23. Are load bearing members free from rot or insect damage?   Yes   No   N/A

24. Are wood members free from checks more than 24" in length and/or 1/4" in width?   Yes   No   N/A

25. If a wood preservative was used on the structure, list the preservative's name:_____ .

26. Is the wood preservative safe for use in children's play areas?   Yes   No   N/A

27. If a wood preservative was used, has a sealant been applied to treated areas every two years?   Yes   No   N/A

For Metal:

28. If it is steel, is it galvanized or powder coated?   Yes   No   N/A

29. If it is aluminum, is it powder coated or anodized?   Yes   No   N/A

30. Is the equipment free from rust on steel, corrosion on aluminum, or peeling paint?   Yes   No   N/A

For Plastic:

31. Are plastic parts unbroken and without chips or cracks, particularly at joints and connections?   Yes   No   N/A

For Paint:

32. If equipment was painted, was paint without lead used?   Yes   No   N/A

PARK NAME	DATE OF INSPECTION	INSPECTOR

SITE BUILT EQUIPMENT ACCESSIBILITY

33. Is the equipment accessible to individuals with the following disabilities (please check all that apply):　　　Yes　　No　　N/A

❏ Wheelchair Users　　　　　　❏ Cane/Crutch/Walker Users
❏ Developmentally Disabled　　❏ Hearing Impaired
❏ Visually Impaired　　　　　　❏ Emotional/Behavioral Disability

34. Is there a way to make this piece usable by a greater number of people with disabilities? (Please specify.)　　Yes　　No　　N/A

_____

_____

_____

_____

_____

_____

35. Can the equipment be adapted without creating a safety hazard for others?　　Yes　　No　　N/A

36. Can a person using a wheelchair, cane, crutches or other assistive device approach the equipment?　　Yes　　No　　N/A

37. Are clear sight lines provided from the top to the bottom of the equipment and from the equipment to adult supervision areas?　　Yes　　No　　N/A

38. Is the equipment easily understood?　　Yes　　No　　N/A

39. Does elevated equipment provide more than one means of exit of varying degrees of difficulty?　　Yes　　No　　N/A

PARK NAME

DATE OF INSPECTION

INSPECTOR

Hazards are apparent from this inspection:

❏ Repair the problem,
❏ Submit a work order,
❏ Barricade or close the area, or
❏ Notify your supervisor.
❏ _____

SITE BUILT EQUIPMENT SAFETY RECOMMENDATIONS

❏ No Hazardous Conditions Found
❏ Removal/Repair Necessary (Prepare Work Order)

WORK ORDER

Item	Action	Date Completed	Time Spent	Cost ($)

SITE BUILT EQUIPMENT ACCESSIBILITY RECOMMENDATIONS

Item	Action	Date Completed	Time Spent	Cost ($)

SLIDES

PARK NAME

DATE OF INSPECTION

INSPECTOR

TYPE OF SLIDE ______________________________

MANUFACTURER ______________________________

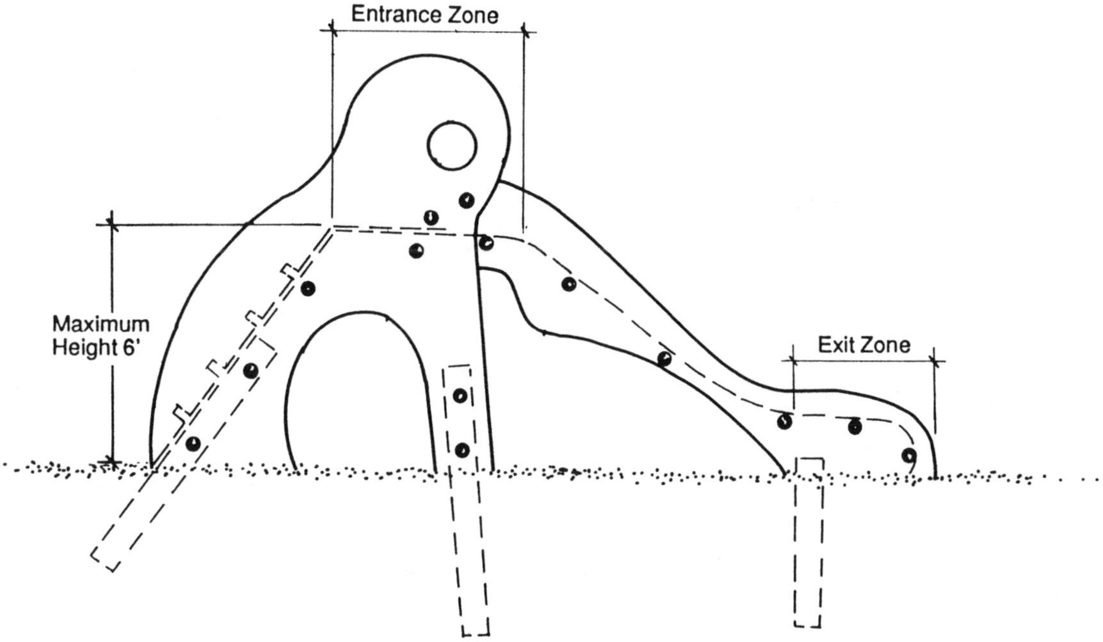
Entrance Zone
Maximum
Height 6'
Exit Zone

PARK NAME	DATE OF INSPECTION	INSPECTOR

If any of these items is answered NO, repair/remove the equipment immediately.

EQUIPMENT CONDITION/HEIGHT/FALL ZONE

1. Is the equipment stable and without severe structural deterioration (e.g., at footings and joints)? Yes   No   N/A

2. Does the equipment have an 8' obstruction-free fall zone in front of the exit region and a 6' obstruction-free fall zone on all other sides? Yes   No   N/A

3. Is the slide height 6' or less? Yes   No   N/A

4. Is there a double rail or vinyl coated chain across the entry to the sliding surface? Yes   No   N/A

5. Is the average slope of the slide 30° or less with no incline greater than 45°? Yes   No   N/A

ENTRAPMENT

6. Are all openings smaller than 3/8" or greater than 1" to prevent finger entrapment? Yes   No   N/A

7. Are the bedway support frames straight and undamaged and do not form a finger entrapment? Yes   No   N/A

8. Are openings smaller than 3" or larger than 9" to prevent head entrapment? Yes   No   N/A

9. Are angles greater than 55° to prevent head entrapment? Yes   No   N/A

GENERAL CONSIDERATIONS

10. Is the equipment complete without missing parts, free of vandalism which would impair safe use, and has no warping or bending of members. Yes   No   N/A

PARK NAME	DATE OF INSPECTION	INSPECTOR

11. If the slide is over 30" in height, does it have an entry platform at least 10" in length and as wide as the inclined surface?   Yes   No   N/A

12. If the slide is over 30" in height, does it have protective barriers which meet the following dimensions (see drawing):   Yes   No   N/A

> P = 38" minimum
> R = 10" minimum
> T = 21" minimum
> S = 14" minimum

13. If the slide is over 4' in height, does it meet the following requirements:

   a.   Is the length of the exit zone a minimum of 16" long?   Yes   No   N/A

   b.   Is the height of the exit zone between 9" and 15" from the ground?   Yes   No   N/A

   c.   Is the slope of the exit zone between 0° and 4° below horizontal?   Yes   No   N/A

   d.   Is the radius of curvature in the exit zone at least 30°?   Yes   No   N/A

14. Do the slide chute rails extend 2-1/2" above the sliding surface?   Yes   No   N/A

15. Is the slide of one piece construction or are the pieces connected by lap joints rather than butt joints?   Yes   No   N/A

16. If the slide is enclosed, is the interior diameter not less than 24" or greater than 30"?   Yes   No   N/A

17. Are there clear sight lines from the top to the bottom of the slide?   Yes   No   N/A

PARK NAME	DATE OF INSPECTION	INSPECTOR

18. Is the equipment free from pinch or crush points? Yes No N/A

19. Is the equipment free from sharp points, corners, or edges? Yes No N/A

20. Is the equipment free from any protrusions (all nuts and bolts are recessed, fitted with tamper proof locks and the holes plugged)? Yes No N/A

21. Is the equipment free from suspended cables, wires, or ropes which would allow a rapidly moving child to impact his head or neck? Yes No N/A

22. Is the slide surface smooth and appropriate for children? Yes No N/A

23. If the slide is stainless steel, is it installed in a northerly direction or have adequate shading? Yes No N/A

24. Are the tops of concrete footings buried 12" below the ground level? Yes No N/A

25. Is the scale of the equipment appropriate to the size of the users? Yes No N/A

LADDERS

26. Are slide stairs fully enclosed and do not trap surfacing material or form a finger entrapment? Yes No N/A

27. Do ladders with steps have a slope of 50° – 75°? Yes No N/A

28. Do stairways have a slope no greater than 35°? Yes No N/A

29. Are steps horizontal plus or minus 2°? Yes No N/A

30. Are steps at least 15" wide? Yes No N/A

31. Are enclosed steps evenly spaced and between 7" and 11" apart? (Measure between the top surface of two consecutive steps) Yes No N/A

PARK NAME	DATE OF INSPECTION	INSPECTOR

32. Is the stair tread depth adequate?   Yes   No   N/A
    (3" or more for open risers; 6" or more for closed risers)

33. Do stairways and ladders with steps have continuous hand   Yes   No   N/A
    rails on both sides designed to maintain the user in an
    upright position?

34. Is the step finish slip resistent?   Yes   No   N/A

HARDWARE

35. Is all hardware present, securely attached, and without   Yes   No   N/A
    significant wear or evidence of deformation?

36. Do fasteners and connecting devices require tools to   Yes   No   N/A
    loosen or remove them (i.e., no hex head bolts or nails are
    used)?

STRUCTURAL MATERIALS

The structure is made of _____ .

For Wood:

37. Are load bearing members free from rot or insect damage?   Yes   No   N/A

38. Are wood members free from checks more than 24" in   Yes   No   N/A
    length and/or 1/4" in width?

39. If a wood preservative was used on the structure, list the
    preservative's name:_____ .

40. Is the wood preservative safe for use in children's play   Yes   No   N/A
    areas?

41. If a wood preservative was used, has a sealant been   Yes   No   N/A
    applied to treated areas every two years?

PARK NAME	DATE OF INSPECTION	INSPECTOR

For Metal:

42. If it is steel, is it galvanized or powder coated?   Yes   No   N/A

43. If it is aluminum, is it powder coated or anodized?   Yes   No   N/A

44. Is the equipment free from rust on steel, corrosion on aluminum, or peeling paint?   Yes   No   N/A

For Plastic:

45. Are plastic parts unbroken and without chips or cracks, particularly at joints and connections?   Yes   No   N/A

For Paint:

46. If equipment was painted, was paint without lead used?   Yes   No   N/A

PARK NAME	DATE OF INSPECTION	INSPECTOR

SLIDE ACCESSIBILITY

47. Is the equipment accessible to individuals with the following disabilities (please check all that apply):   Yes   No   N/A

   ❏ Wheelchair Users   ❏ Cane/Crutch/Walker Users
   ❏ Developmentally Disabled   ❏ Hearing Impaired
   ❏ Visually Impaired   ❏ Emotional/Behavioral Disability

48. Is there a way to make this piece usable by a greater number of people with disabilities? (Please specify.)   Yes   No   N/A

   _____

   _____

   _____

   _____

   _____

   _____

49. Can the equipment be adapted without creating a safety hazard for others?   Yes   No   N/A

50. Can a person using a wheelchair, cane, crutches or other assistive device approach the equipment?   Yes   No   N/A

51. Are clear sight lines provided from the top to the bottom of the equipment and from the equipment to adult supervision areas?   Yes   No   N/A

52. Is the equipment easily understood?   Yes   No   N/A

53. Does elevated equipment provide more than one means of exit of varying degrees of difficulty?   Yes   No   N/A

PARK NAME

DATE OF INSPECTION

INSPECTOR

Hazards are apparent from this inspection:

❑ Repair the problem,
❑ Submit a work order,
❑ Barricade or close the area, or
❑ Notify your supervisor.
❑ _____

SLIDE SAFETY RECOMMENDATIONS

❑ No Hazardous Conditions Found
❑ Removal/Repair Necessary (Prepare Work Order)

WORK ORDER

Item	Action	Date Completed	Time Spent	Cost ($)

SLIDE ACCESSIBILITY RECOMMENDATIONS

Item	Action	Date Completed	Time Spent	Cost ($)

PARK NAME

DATE OF INSPECTION

INSPECTOR

MANUFACTURER _____.

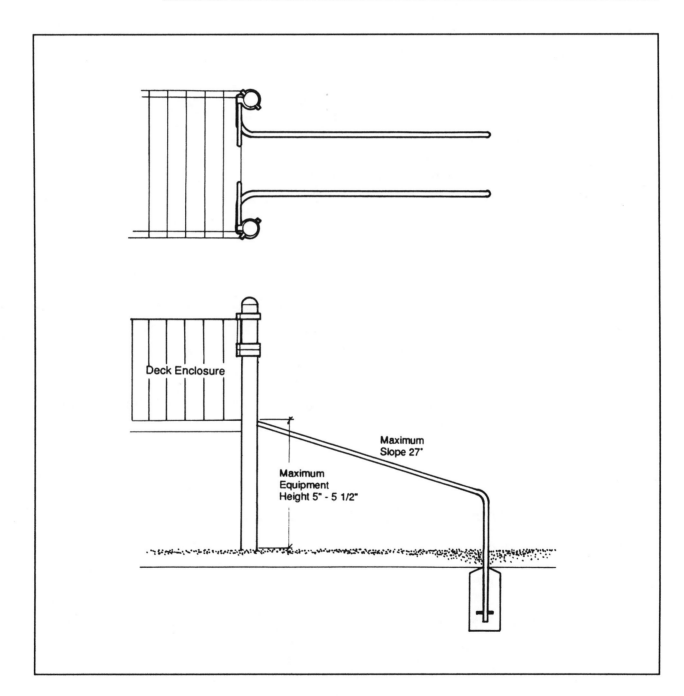

Deck Enclosure

Maximum
Slope 27°

Maximum
Equipment
Height 5" - 5 1/2"

PARK NAME

DATE OF INSPECTION

INSPECTOR

If any of these items is answered NO, repair/remove the equipment immediately.

EQUIPMENT CONDITION/HEIGHT/FALL ZONE

1.	Is the equipment stable and without severe structural deterioration (e.g., at footings and joints)?	Yes	No	N/A
2.	Does the equipment have an 8' obstruction-free fall zone?	Yes	No	N/A
3.	Is the height 66" or less?	Yes	No	N/A
4.	For banister slides, is the average incline 27° or less?	Yes	No	N/A

ENTRAPMENT

5.	Are all openings smaller than 3/8" or greater than 1" to prevent finger entrapment?	Yes	No	N/A
6.	Are the support frames straight, undamaged and do not form a finger entrapment?	Yes	No	N/A
7.	Are openings smaller than 3" or larger than 9" to prevent head entrapment?	Yes	No	N/A
8.	Are angles greater than 55° to prevent head entrapment?	Yes	No	N/A

GENERAL CONSIDERATIONS

9.	Is the equipment complete without missing parts, free of vandalism which would impair safe use, and has no warping or bending of members.	Yes	No	N/A
10.	Is the pole diameter between 1-3/4" and 2-1/2"?	Yes	No	N/A
11.	Do rails support a child's transition to sliding?	Yes	No	N/A
12.	Are there clear sight lines from the top to the bottom of the slide?	Yes	No	N/A
13.	Is the equipment free from pinch or crush points?	Yes	No	N/A

PARK NAME

DATE OF INSPECTION

INSPECTOR

14. Is the equipment free from sharp points, corners, or edges?　　Yes　No　N/A

15. Is the equipment free from any protrusions (all nuts and bolts are recessed, fitted with tamper proof locks and the holes plugged)?　　Yes　No　N/A

16. Is the equipment free from suspended cables, wires, or ropes which would allow a rapidly moving child to impact his head or neck?　　Yes　No　N/A

17. Is the pole surface smooth and appropriate for sliding?　　Yes　No　N/A

18. Are the tops of concrete footings buried 12" below the ground level?　　Yes　No　N/A

19. Is the scale of the equipment appropriate to the size of the users?　　Yes　No　N/A

HARDWARE

20. Is all hardware present, securely attached, and without significant wear or evidence of deformation?　　Yes　No　N/A

21. Do fasteners and connecting devices require tools to loosen or remove them (i.e., no hex head bolts or nails are used)?　　Yes　No　N/A

PARK NAME

DATE OF INSPECTION

INSPECTOR

STRUCTURAL MATERIALS

The structure is made of _____ .

For Wood:

22. Are load bearing members free from rot or insect damage?   Yes   No   N/A

23. Are wood members free from checks more than 24" in
    length and/or 1/4" in width?   Yes   No   N/A

24. If a wood preservative was used on the structure, list the
    preservative's name:_____ .

25. Is the wood preservative safe for use in children's play
    areas?   Yes   No   N/A

26. If a wood preservative was used, has a sealant been
    applied to treated areas every two years?   Yes   No   N/A

For Metal:

27. If it is steel, is it galvanized or powder coated?   Yes   No   N/A

28. If it is aluminum, is it powder coated or anodized?   Yes   No   N/A

29. Is the equipment free from rust on steel, corrosion on
    aluminum, or peeling paint?   Yes   No   N/A

For Paint:

30. If equipment was painted, was paint without lead used?   Yes   No   N/A

PARK NAME

DATE OF INSPECTION

INSPECTOR

SLIDE ACCESSIBILITY

31. Is the equipment accessible to individuals with the following disabilities (please check all that apply):   Yes   No   N/A

□ Wheelchair Users   □ Cane/Crutch/Walker Users
□ Developmentally Disabled   □ Hearing Impaired
□ Visually Impaired   □ Emotional/Behavioral Disability

32. Is there a way to make this piece usable by a greater number of people with disabilities? (Please specify.)   Yes   No   N/A

_____

_____

_____

_____

_____

_____

33. Can the equipment be adapted without creating a safety hazard for others?   Yes   No   N/A

34. Can a person using a wheelchair, cane, crutches or other assistive device approach the equipment?   Yes   No   N/A

35. Are clear sight lines provided from the top to the bottom of the equipment and from the equipment to adult supervision areas?   Yes   No   N/A

36. Is the equipment easily understood?   Yes   No   N/A

37. Does elevated equipment provide more than one means of exit of varying degrees of difficulty?   Yes   No   N/A

BANNISTER SLIDE RECOMMENDATIONS   17C

PARK NAME	DATE OF INSPECTION	INSPECTOR

Hazards are apparent from this inspection:

- ❑ Repair the problem,
- ❑ Submit a work order,
- ❑ Barricade or close the area, or
- ❑ Notify your supervisor.
- ❑ _____

BANNISTER SLIDE SAFETY RECOMMENDATIONS

- ❑ No Hazardous Conditions Found
- ❑ Removal/Repair Necessary (Prepare Work Order)

WORK ORDER

Item	Action	Date Completed	Time Spent	Cost ($)

BANNISTER SLIDE ACCESSIBILITY RECOMMENDATIONS

Item	Action	Date Completed	Time Spent	Cost ($)

PARK NAME

DATE OF INSPECTION

INSPECTOR

MANUFACTURER _____

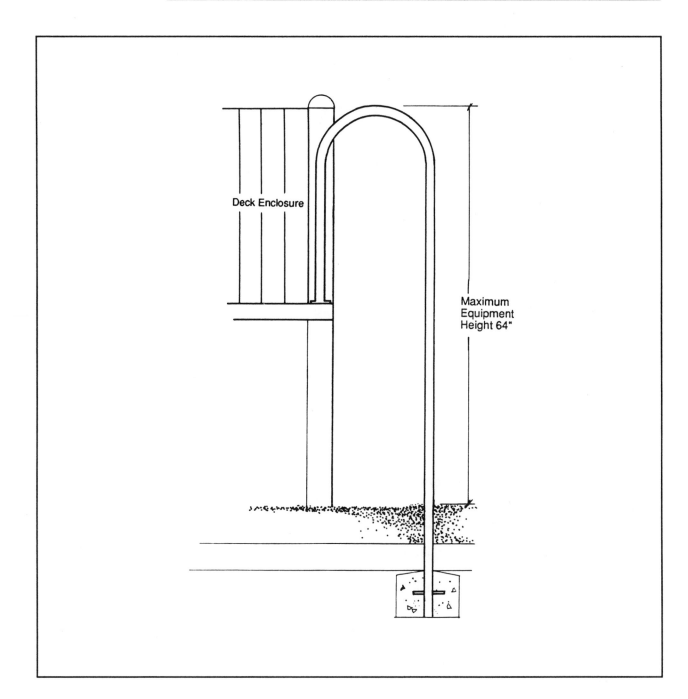

Deck Enclosure

Maximum Equipment Height 64"

PARK NAME	DATE OF INSPECTION	INSPECTOR

If any of these items is answered NO, repair/remove the equipment immediately.

EQUIPMENT CONDITION/HEIGHT/FALL ZONE

1. Is the equipment stable and without severe structural deterioration (e.g., at footings and joints)?   Yes   No   N/A

2. Does the equipment have an 8' obstruction-free fall zone?   Yes   No   N/A

3. Is the height 64" or less?   Yes   No   N/A

ENTRAPMENT

4. Are all openings smaller than 3/8" or greater than 1" to prevent finger entrapment?   Yes   No   N/A

5. Are the support frames straight, undamaged and do not form a finger entrapment?   Yes   No   N/A

6. Are openings smaller than 3" or larger than 9" to prevent head entrapment?   Yes   No   N/A

7. Are angles greater than 55° to prevent head entrapment?   Yes   No   N/A

GENERAL CONSIDERATIONS

8. Is the equipment complete without missing parts, free of vandalism which would impair safe use, and has no warping or bending of members.   Yes   No   N/A

9. Is the pole diameter between 1-3/4" and 2-1/2"?   Yes   No   N/A

10. Do rails support a child's transition to sliding?   Yes   No   N/A

11. Are there clear sight lines from the top to the bottom of the slide?   Yes   No   N/A

12. Is the circulation space under the fire pole deck blocked to prevent entrance to the fire pole fall zone?   Yes   No   N/A

PARK NAME	DATE OF INSPECTION	INSPECTOR

13. Is the equipment free from pinch or crush points? Yes No N/A

14. Is the equipment free from sharp points, corners, or edges? Yes No N/A

15. Is the equipment free from any protrusions (all nuts and bolts are recessed, fitted with tamper proof locks and the holes plugged)? Yes No N/A

16. Is the equipment free from suspended cables, wires, or ropes which would allow a rapidly moving child to impact his head or neck? Yes No N/A

17. Is the pole surface smooth and appropriate for sliding? Yes No N/A

18. Are the tops of concrete footings buried 12" below the ground level? Yes No N/A

19. Is the scale of the equipment appropriate to the size of the users? Yes No N/A

HARDWARE

20. Is all hardware present, securely attached, and without significant wear or evidence of deformation? Yes No N/A

21. Do fasteners and connecting devices require tools to loosen or remove them (i.e., no hex head bolts or nails are used)? Yes No N/A

PARK NAME

DATE OF INSPECTION

INSPECTOR

STRUCTURAL MATERIALS

The structure is made of _____.

For Wood:

22. Are load bearing members free from rot or insect damage?   Yes   No   N/A

23. Are wood members free from checks more than 24" in length and/or 1/4" in width?   Yes   No   N/A

24. If a wood preservative was used on the structure, list the preservatives name:_____.

25. Is the wood preservative safe for use in children's play areas?   Yes   No   N/A

26. If a wood preservative was used, has a sealant been applied to treated areas every two years?   Yes   No   N/A

For Metal:

27. If it is steel, is it galvanized or powder coated?   Yes   No   N/A

28. If it is aluminum, is it powder coated or anodized?   Yes   No   N/A

29. Is the equipment free from rust on steel, corrosion on aluminum, or peeling paint?   Yes   No   N/A

For Paint:

30. IIf equipment was painted, was paint without lead used?   Yes   No   N/A

PARK NAME	DATE OF INSPECTION	INSPECTOR

SLIDE ACCESSIBILITY

31. Is the equipment accessible to individuals with the following disabilities (please check all that apply):   Yes   No   N/A

   ❑ Wheelchair Users   ❑ Cane/Crutch/Walker Users

   ❑ Developmentally Disabled   ❑ Hearing Impaired

   ❑ Visually Impaired   ❑ Emotional/Behavioral Disability

32. Is there a way to make this piece usable by a greater number of people with disabilities? (Please specify.)   Yes   No   N/A

_____

_____

_____

_____

_____

_____

33. Can the equipment be adapted without creating a safety hazard for others?   Yes   No   N/A

34. Can a person using a wheelchair, cane, crutches or other assistive device approach the equipment?   Yes   No   N/A

35. Are clear sight lines provided from the top to the bottom of the equipment and from the equipment to adult supervision areas?   Yes   No   N/A

36. Is the equipment easily understood?   Yes   No   N/A

37. Does elevated equipment provide more than one means of exit of varying degrees of difficulty?   Yes   No   N/A

FIRE POLE RECOMMENDATIONS   18C

PARK NAME

DATE OF INSPECTION

INSPECTOR

Hazards are apparent from this inspection:

- ❑ Repair the problem,
- ❑ Submit a work order,
- ❑ Barricade or close the area, or
- ❑ Notify your supervisor.
- ❑ _____

FIRE POLE SAFETY RECOMMENDATIONS

- ❑ No Hazardous Conditions Found
- ❑ Removal/Repair Necessary (Prepare Work Order)

WORK ORDER

Item	Action	Date Completed	Time Spent	Cost ($)

FIRE POLE ACCESSIBILITY RECOMMENDATIONS

Item	Action	Date Completed	Time Spent	Cost ($)

PARK NAME

DATE OF INSPECTION

INSPECTOR

MANUFACTURER _____.

Length of
16" Exit Zone

9" - 15"
Exit Zone
Height

PARK NAME	DATE OF INSPECTION	INSPECTOR

If any of these items is answered NO, repair/remove the equipment immediately.

EQUIPMENT CONDITION/HEIGHT/FALL ZONE

1. Is the equipment stable and without severe structural deterioration (e.g., at footings and joints)?   Yes   No   N/A

2. Does the slide have a 8' obstruction free fall zone in front of the exit region and a 6' obstruction free fall zone on all other sides over 30" off the ground?   Yes   No   N/A

3. Is the slide higher than 6' from surface level?   Yes   No   N/A

4. Is there a bike barrier at the top of the slide?   Yes   No   N/A

5. Is there a double rail or vinyl coated chain across the entry to the sliding surface?   Yes   No   N/A

6. Is there a bicycle barrier at the bottom of the slide?   Yes   No   N/A

ENTRAPMENT

7. Are all openings smaller than 3/8" or greater than 1" to prevent finger entrapment?   Yes   No   N/A

8. Are openings smaller than 3" or larger than 9" to prevent head entrapment?   Yes   No   N/A

9. Are angles greater than 55° to prevent head entrapment?   Yes   No   N/A

GENERAL CONSIDERATIONS

10. Is the equipment complete without missing parts, free of vandalism which would impair safe use, and has no warping or bending of members.   Yes   No   N/A

11. Is there a staging platform at the top of the slide?   Yes   No   N/A

12. Is erosion present on the side of the hill?   Yes   No   N/A

PARK NAME	DATE OF INSPECTION	INSPECTOR

13. Are there steps or a trail to the top of the slide? Yes No N/A

14. Is the stairway/trail free from trip hazards and steep grades and are handrails provided on both sides? Yes No N/A

15. Are the slide and hill well maintained? Yes No N/A

16. Are the bedway support frames straight, undamaged and do not form a finger entrapment? Yes No N/A

17. Is the average incline of the sliding surface 30° or less with no incline greater than 45°? Yes No N/A

18. If the slide is over 30" in height, does it have protective barriers which meet the following dimensions: Yes No N/A

      P = 38" minimum
      R = 10" minimum
      T = 21" minimum
      S = 14" minimum

19. If the slide is over 4' in height, does it meet the following requirements:

    a. Is the length of the exit zone a minimum of 16" long? Yes No N/A

    b. Is the height of the exit zone between 9" and 15" above ground level? Yes No N/A

    c. Is the slope of the exit zone between 0° and 4° below horizon? Yes No N/A

    d. Is the radius of curvature in the exit zone at least 30°? Yes No N/A

20. Do the slide chute rails extend 2-1/2" above the sliding surface? Yes No N/A

21. Does the width of the slide chute rails allow children to easily grip them? Yes No N/A

PARK NAME

DATE OF INSPECTION

INSPECTOR

23. If the slide is enclosed, is the interior diameter not less than 24" or greater than 30"?　　Yes　No　N/A

24. Is the equipment free from pinch or crush points?　　Yes　No　N/A

25. Is the equipment free from sharp points, corners, or edges?　　Yes　No　N/A

26. Is the equipment free from any protrusions (all nuts and bolts are recessed, fitted with tamper proof locks and the holes plugged)?　　Yes　No　N/A

27. Is the equipment free from suspended cables, wires, or ropes which would allow a rapidly moving child to impact his head or neck?　　Yes　No　N/A

28. Is the slide surface smooth and appropriate for children?　　Yes　No　N/A

29. If the slide is stainless steel, is it installed in a northerly direction or have adequate shading?　　Yes　No　N/A

30. Are the tops of concrete footings buried below the ground level?　　Yes　No　N/A

31. Is the scale of the equipment appropriate to the size of the users?　　Yes　No　N/A

HARDWARE

32. Is all hardware present, securely attached, and without significant wear or evidence of deformation?　　Yes　No　N/A

33. Do fasteners and connecting devices require tools to loosen or remove them (i.e., no hex head bolts or nails are used)?　　Yes　No　N/A

PARK NAME	DATE OF INSPECTION	INSPECTOR

STRUCTURAL MATERIALS

The structure is made of _____.
(Concrete is not acceptable.)

For Wood:

34. Are load bearing members free from rot or insect damage?　　Yes　No　N/A

35. Are wood members free from checks more than 24" in length and/or 1/4" in width?　　Yes　No　N/A

36. If a wood preservative was used on the structure, list the preservatives name:_____.

37. Is the wood preservative safe for use in children's play areas?　　Yes　No　N/A

38. If a wood preservative was used, has a sealant been applied to treated areas every two years?　　Yes　No　N/A

For Metal:

39. If it is steel, is it galvanized or powder coated?　　Yes　No　N/A

40. If it is aluminum, is it powder coated or anodized?　　Yes　No　N/A

41. Is the equipment free from rust on steel, corrosion on aluminum, or peeling paint?　　Yes　No　N/A

For Plastic:

42. Are plastic parts unbroken and without chips or cracks, particularly at joints and connections?　　Yes　No　N/A

For Paint:

43. If equipment was painted, was paint without lead used?　　Yes　No　N/A

PARK NAME	DATE OF INSPECTION	INSPECTOR

HILL SLIDE ACCESSIBILITY

44. Is the equipment accessible to individuals with the following disabilities (please check all that apply):   Yes   No   N/A

   ❑ Wheelchair Users   ❑ Cane/Crutch/Walker Users
   ❑ Developmentally Disabled   ❑ Hearing Impaired
   ❑ Visually Impaired   ❑ Emotional/Behavioral Disability

45. Is there a way to make this piece usable by a greater number of people with disabilities? (Please specify.)   Yes   No   N/A

   _____

   _____

   _____

   _____

   _____

   _____

46. Can the equipment be adapted without creating a safety hazard for others?   Yes   No   N/A

47. Can a person using a wheelchair, cane, crutches or other assistive device approach the equipment?   Yes   No   N/A

48. Are clear sight lines provided from the top to the bottom of the equipment and from the equipment to adult supervision areas?   Yes   No   N/A

49. Is the equipment easily understood?   Yes   No   N/A

50. Does elevated equipment provide more than one means of exit of varying degrees of difficulty?   Yes   No   N/A

PARK NAME

DATE OF INSPECTION

INSPECTOR

Hazards are apparent from this inspection:

❑ Repair the problem,
❑ Submit a work order,
❑ Barricade or close the area, or
❑ Notify your supervisor.
❑ _____

HILL SLIDE SAFETY RECOMMENDATIONS

❑ No Hazardous Conditions Found
❑ Removal/Repair Necessary (Prepare Work Order)

WORK ORDER

Item	Action	Date Completed	Time Spent	Cost ($)

HILL SLIDE ACCESSIBILITY RECOMMENDATIONS

Item	Action	Date Completed	Time Spent	Cost ($)

PARK NAME

DATE OF INSPECTION

INSPECTOR

Manufacturer _____

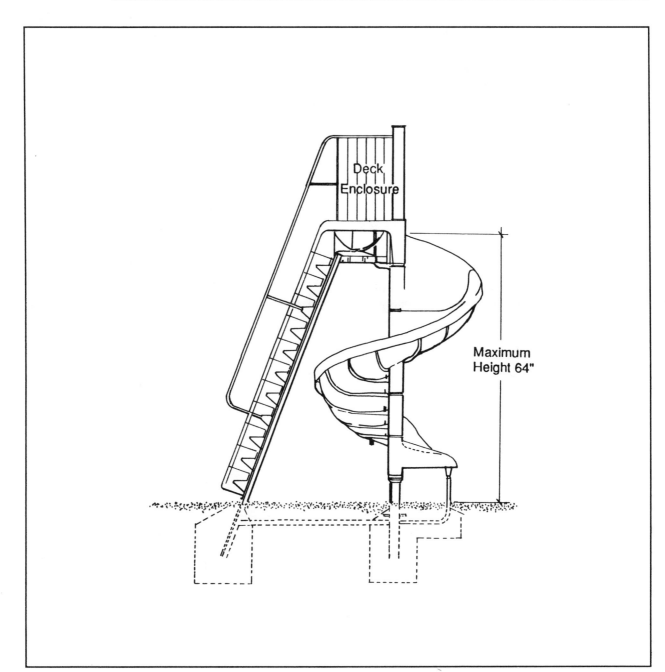

PARK NAME

DATE OF INSPECTION

INSPECTOR

If any of these items is answered NO, repair/remove the equipment immediately.

EQUIPMENT CONDITION/HEIGHT/FALL ZONE

1. Is the equipment stable and without severe structural deterioration (e.g., at footings and joints)?   Yes   No   N/A

2. Does the equipment have an 8' obstruction-free fall zone in front of the exit region and a 6' obstruction-free fall zone on all other sides?   Yes   No   N/A

3. Is the outside slide chute rail at least 2.5 inches high?   Yes   No   N/A

4. Are there clear sight lines from the top to the bottom of the slide?   Yes   No   N/A

5. To determine the maximum vertical drop of the curved section, or height of the slide chute (H), measure the vertical distance between the entrance to the slide and the lowest point on the spiral section of the chute.

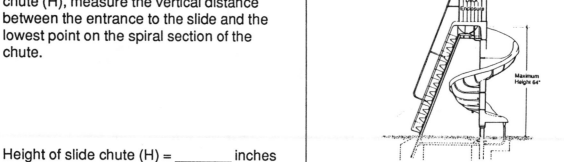

Height of slide chute (H) = _____ inches

6. Is the maximum spiral height under 64"?   Yes   No   N/A

If any of the above items are answered NO, the equipment is unsafe. Do not continue the survey.

PARK NAME   DATE OF INSPECTION   INSPECTOR

Continue the survey only if questions 1 - 6 were answered YES.

The potential for falling over the side of a spiral slide is a function of the height of the slide bed, the banking angle of the slide bed, the radius of the spiral, and the height of the slide chute rail.

To be safe, the slide chute rail must be high enough to hold the child in the given banking angle. Use the calculations and charts on the following pages to determine whether or not the slide has an appropriate rail height. If the height of the side rails are lower than those specified on the chart, the slide is not safe.

You will find the following simple tools helpful in completing this part of your safety inspection. You will find directions for their construction in Part II, "Inspection Tool Kit."

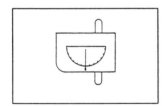

Curve Gauge
Determines the potential means of falling from a spiral slide bed.

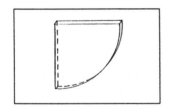

Abrupt Angle Slide Rule
Determines the banking angle and radius of slide beds where there is the potential of **tipping** over the outer slide chute rail.

Continuous Curve Slide Rule
Determines the banking angle and radius of slide beds where there is the potential for **sliding** over the outer slide chute rail.

PARK NAME	DATE OF INSPECTION	INSPECTOR

FALLING OVER THE OUTER EDGE

There are two ways in which a child can fall over the outer edge of a spiral slide: by **tipping** out of the bedway or by **sliding** off the bedway.

> Tipping = an ABRUPT bedway angle.
> Sliding = a CONTINUAL bedway angle.

7. Use the curve gauge to determine whether the slide bedway angle is ABRUPT or CONTINUOUS. To use the curve gauge, place the curved edge of the tool against the angle formed by the slide chute rail and the slide bed. If both corners of the curved edge make contact with the slide in this position, the slide has an abrupt angle. If only one corner of the curved edge makes contact with the slide in this position, the slide has a continuous curve.

The angle formed by the slide chute rail and the slide bed is (check one):

❏ an ABRUPT ANGLE.

   Go to Question 8.

❏ a CONTINUOUS ANGLE.

   Go to Question 12.

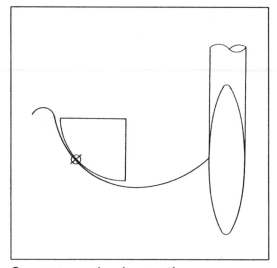

Curve gauge showing **abrupt angle** and two-point contact with the chute.

Curve gauge showing **continuous curve** and one-point contact with the chute.

PARK NAME	DATE OF INSPECTION	INSPECTOR

Abrupt Spiral Slide Angle

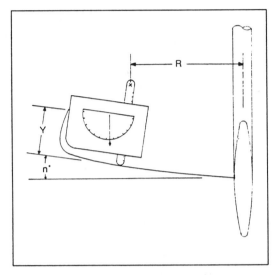

Using the Abrupt Angle Slide Rule

8. If the angle of the spiral slide is ABRUPT, use the abrupt angle slide rule to determine the radius and banking angle of the slide chute (see illustration) and record those figures here.

    To use the the abrupt angle slide rule, position it against the outer slide chute rail and adjust the sliding scale so that the base of the slide rule is parallel to the slide bed. Measure the radius (R) from the X on the top of the sliding scale to the center of the spiral center pole; measure the banking angle (n°) by reading the angle on the protractor. The banking angle equals 90° minus the angle indicated on the protractor by the weight and string.

    Radius (R) = _____ inches

    Banking Angle (n°) = _____ degrees

9. With a ruler or tape measure, measure the height of the outer edge (Y).

    Measured Outer Edge (Y) = _____ inches

    In no case should the outer edge be less than 2.5 inches.

    Is the height of the outer edge 2.5 inches or greater?   Yes   No   N/A

    If NO, the slide is not safe and should be removed or replaced. If YES, continue on.

10. Calculate the Minimum Effective Edge Height using the charts on the following page. Locate the chart for the radius (R) that most closely matches the radius of the slide chute measured in Question 8. Using the height (H) that most closely matches the height of the spiral slide chute measured in Question 5, read across the chart, locating the minimum effective edge height (Y) for the banking angle (n°, from Question 8).

Minimum Effective Edge Height (Y) = _____ inches

Example:

Given a slide with a spiral height of 60 inches, a spiral radius of 21 inches and a banking angle of 25 degrees, the minimum effective edge height is 4.5 inches.

11. Does the measured edge height from Question 9 equal or exceed the minimum effective edge height as calculated in Question 10?

Yes   No   N/A

If NO, the slide is not safe and should be removed or replaced. If YES, continue on.

PARK NAME

DATE OF INSPECTION

INSPECTOR

R = Radius of Slide Spiral in Inches
H = Height of Slide Chute in Inches
n° = Banking Angle in Degrees

R = 12"

H	0°	5°	10°	15°	20°	25°	30°	35°	40°
36"	8.1	7.5	6.9	6.2	5.5	4.6	3.7	2.6	
48"	8.5	7.9	7.3	6.6	5.9	5.1	4.3	3.3	
60"	8.7	8.1	7.5	6.9	6.2	5.4	4.6	3.6	2.5
72"	8.8	8.2	7.6	7.0	6.3	5.6	4.8	3.9	2.8

R = 15"

H	0°	5°	10°	15°	20°	25°	30°	35°	40°
36"	7.8	7.2	6.5	5.8	5.0	4.1	3.1		
48"	8.2	7.6	7.0	6.3	5.6	4.8	3.8	2.8	
60"	8.5	7.9	7.3	6.6	5.9	5.1	4.3	3.3	
72"	8.7	8.1	7.5	6.8	6.1	5.4	4.5	3.6	

R = 18"

H	0°	5°	10°	15°	20°	25°	30°	35°	40°
36"	7.5	6.8	6.1	5.4	4.5	3.6			
48"	8.0	7.4	6.7	6.0	5.2	4.4	3.4		
60"	8.3	7.7	7.1	6.4	5.7	4.8	3.9	2.9	
72"	8.5	7.9	7.3	6.6	5.9	5.1	4.3	3.3	

R = 21"

H	0°	5°	10°	15°	20°	25°	30°	35°	40°
36"	7.1	6.5	5.7	4.9	4.0	3.0			
48"	7.7	7.1	6.4	5.7	4.9	4.0	2.9		
60"	8.1	7.5	6.8	6.1	5.4	4.5	3.6		
72"	8.3	7.7	7.1	6.4	5.7	4.9	4.0	2.9	

R = 24"

H	0°	5°	10°	15°	20°	25°	30°	35°	40°
36"	6.8	6.1	5.3	4.5	3.5				
48"	7.5	6.8	6.1	5.4	4.5	3.6			
60"	7.9	7.3	6.6	5.9	5.1	4.2	3.2		
72"	8.1	7.5	6.9	6.2	5.5	4.6	3.7	2.6	

Minimum Effective Edge Height Charts – 'Y' Inches

(Refer to Question 10)

PARK NAME   DATE OF INSPECTION   INSPECTOR

Continuous Curve Spiral Slide Angle

12. If the angle of the spiral slide is CONTINUOUS, use the continuous curve slide rule to determine the radius and banking angle of the slide chute (see illustration) and record those figures here.

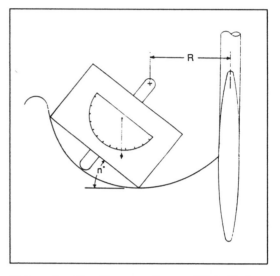

Using the Continuous Curve Slide Rule

To use the the continuous curve slide rule, position it as shown with the base corner nearest the inner edge of the spiral at the low point of the slide bed at any location along the chute. Adjust the sliding scale so that it contacts the bed of the slide. Measure the radius (R) from the X on the top of the sliding scale to the middle of the spiral center pole; measure the banking angle (n°) by reading the angle on the protractor. The banking angle equals 90° minus the angle indicated on the protractor by the weight and string.

Radius (R) = _____ inches

Banking Angle (n°) = _____ degrees

PARK NAME

DATE OF INSPECTION

INSPECTOR

13. To determine the safety of the banking angle, compare the banking angle measured in Question 12 with the Minimum Effective Banking Angle. To find the minimum effective banking angle for a spiral slide, refer to the following Minimum Effective Banking Angle chart below. Find the height (H) that is nearest the height of the slide chute measured in Question 5 and read across to the minimum effective banking angle for the radius (R) nearest the radius measured in Question 12.

Minimum Effective Banking Angle $(n°)$ = _____ degrees

Example:
Given a slide with a spiral height of 60 inches, a spiral radius of 21 inches, the minimum effective banking angle is $67°$.

Minimum Effective Banking Angle $(n°)$

H"	R" 12	15	18	21	24
36"	67	64	62	59	56
48"	70	68	66	64	62
60"	72	70	68	67	65
72"	73	71	70	69	67

14. Is the banking angle measured in Question 12 equal to or greater than the minimum effective banking angle calculated in Question 13?   Yes   No   N/A

If NO, the slide is not safe and should be removed or replaced. If YES, continue on.

PARK NAME	DATE OF INSPECTION	INSPECTOR

FALLING FROM THE INNER EDGE

To prevent falling out of the slide by tipping or sliding over the inner edge, the height of the inner edge of the slide should be no less than 2.5 inches. If the slide has a center post, it can be considered the inner edge.

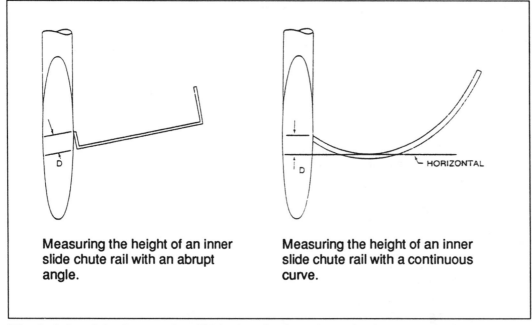

Measuring the height of an inner slide chute rail with an abrupt angle.

Measuring the height of an inner slide chute rail with a continuous curve.

The height of the inner edge (D) is the distance from the lowest point in the slide bed curve and the top of the inner edge.

15. The height of the inner edge (D) is _____ inches

16. Is the height of the inner edge equal to or greater than 2½"?   Yes   No   N/A

**If NO, the slide is not safe and should be removed/replaced.
If YES, continue the safety and access survey using the
survey form for SLIDES.**

SPIRAL SLIDE RECOMMENDATIONS

PARK NAME

DATE OF INSPECTION

INSPECTOR

Hazards are apparent from this inspection:

- ❏ Repair the problem,
- ❏ Submit a work order,
- ❏ Barricade or close the area, or
- ❏ Notify your supervisor.
- ❏ _____

SPIRAL SLIDE SAFETY RECOMMENDATIONS

- ❏ No Hazardous Conditions Found
- ❏ Removal/Repair Necessary (Prepare Work Order)

WORK ORDER

Item	Action	Date Completed	Time Spent	Cost ($)

SPIRAL SLIDE ACCESSIBILITY RECOMMENDATIONS

Item	Action	Date Completed	Time Spent	Cost ($)

PARK NAME

DATE OF INSPECTION

INSPECTOR

MANUFACTURER _____

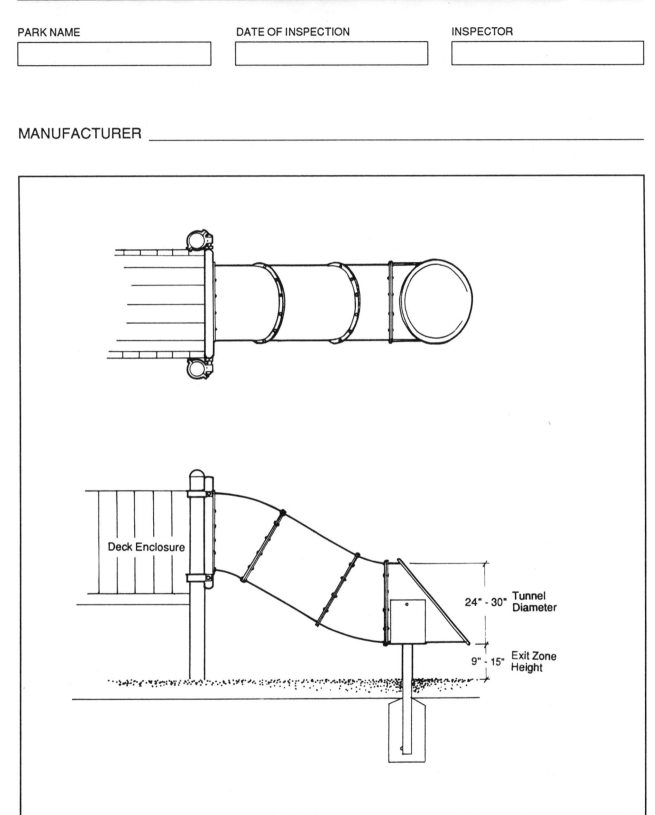

Deck Enclosure

24" - 30" Tunnel Diameter

9" - 15" Exit Zone Height

PARK NAME

DATE OF INSPECTION

INSPECTOR

If any of these items is answered NO, repair/remove the equipment immediately.

EQUIPMENT CONDITION/HEIGHT/FALL ZONE

1. Is the equipment stable and without severe structural deterioration (e.g., at footings and joints)? Yes   No   N/A

2. Does the equipment have an 8' obstruction-free fall zone in front of the exit region and a 6' obstruction-free fall zone on all other sides? Yes   No   N/A

   Yes   No   N/A

3. Is the slide height 6' or less?

4. Is the slope of the slide 30° or less with no incline greater than 45°? Yes   No   N/A

5. Are all tunnel edges rounded? Yes   No   N/A

6. Is the interior diameter not less than 24" or greater than 30"? Yes   No   N/A

ENTRAPMENT

5. Are all openings smaller than 3/8" or greater than 1" to prevent finger entrapment? Yes   No   N/A

6. Are openings smaller than 3" or larger than 9" to prevent head entrapment? Yes   No   N/A

7. Are angles greater than 55° to prevent head entrapment? Yes   No   N/A

GENERAL CONSIDERATIONS

8. Is the equipment complete without missing parts, free of vandalism which would impair safe use, and has no warping or bending of members. Yes   No   N/A

9. If the slide is over 30" in height, does it have an entry platform at least 10" in length and as wide as the inclined surface? Yes   No   N/A

PARK NAME

DATE OF INSPECTION

INSPECTOR

10. If the slide is over 4' in height, does it meet the following requirements:

    a.   Is the length of the exit zone a minimum of 16" long?   Yes   No   N/A

    b.   Is the height of the exit zone between 9" and 15" from the ground?   Yes   No   N/A

    c.   Is the slope of the exit zone between 0° and 4° below horizontal?   Yes   No   N/A

    d.   Is the radius of curvature in the exit zone at least 30°?   Yes   No   N/A

11. Is the slide of one piece construction or are the pieces connected by lap joints rather than butt joints?   Yes   No   N/A

12. Are there clear sight lines from the top to the bottom of the slide?   Yes   No   N/A

13. Is the equipment free from pinch or crush points?   Yes   No   N/A

14. Is the equipment free from sharp points, corners, or edges?   Yes   No   N/A

15. Is the equipment free from any protrusions (all nuts and bolts are recessed, fitted with tamper proof locks and the holes plugged)?   Yes   No   N/A

16. Is the equipment free from suspended cables, wires, or ropes which would allow a rapidly moving child to impact his head or neck?   Yes   No   N/A

17. Is the slide surface smooth and appropriate for children?   Yes   No   N/A

18. If the slide is stainless steel, is it installed in a northerly direction or have adequate shading?   Yes   No   N/A

19. Are all platforms above 30" surrounded by non-climbable protective barriers at least 38" in height?   Yes   No   N/A

20. Are the tops of concrete footings buried 12" below the ground level?   Yes   No   N/A

TUNNEL SLIDE SAFETY 21A

PARK NAME	DATE OF INSPECTION	INSPECTOR

21. Is the scale of the equipment appropriate to the size of the users? Yes   No   N/A

HARDWARE

22. Is all hardware present, securely attached, and without significant wear or evidence of deformation? Yes   No   N/A

23. Do fasteners and connecting devices require tools to loosen or remove them (i.e., no hex head bolts or nails are used)? Yes   No   N/A

STRUCTURAL MATERIALS

The structure is made of _____ .

For Wood:

24. Are load bearing members free from rot or insect damage? Yes   No   N/A

25. Are wood members free from checks more than 24" in length and/or 1/4" in width? Yes   No   N/A

26. If a wood preservative was used on the structure, list the preservatives name:_____ .

27. Is the wood preservative safe for use in children's play areas? Yes   No   N/A

28. If a wood preservative was used, has a sealant been applied to treated areas every two years? Yes   No   N/A

For Metal:

29. If it is steel, is it galvanized or powder coated? Yes   No   N/A

30. If it is aluminum, is it powder coated or anodized? Yes   No   N/A

31. Is the equipment free from rust on steel, corrosion on aluminum, or peeling paint? Yes   No   N/A

©1989, MIG Communications

PARK NAME

DATE OF INSPECTION

INSPECTOR

For Plastic:

32. Are plastic parts unbroken and without chips or cracks,
particularly at joints and connections?   Yes   No   N/A

For Paint:

33. If equipment was painted, was paint without lead used?   Yes   No   N/A

PARK NAME

DATE OF INSPECTION

INSPECTOR

TUNNEL SLIDE ACCESSIBILITY

		Yes	No	N/A
34.	Is the equipment accessible to individuals with the following disabilities (please check all that apply):			

- ❏ Wheelchair Users
- ❏ Developmentally Disabled
- ❏ Visually Impaired
- ❏ Cane/Crutch/Walker Users
- ❏ Hearing Impaired
- ❏ Emotional/Behavioral Disability

35. Is there a way to make this piece usable by a greater number of people with disabilities? (Please specify.)   Yes   No   N/A

_____

_____

_____

_____

_____

_____

36. Can the equipment be adapted without creating a safety hazard for others?   Yes   No   N/A

37. Can a person using a wheelchair, cane, crutches or other assistive device approach the equipment?   Yes   No   N/A

38. Are clear sight lines provided from the top to the bottom of the equipment and from the equipment to adult supervision areas?   Yes   No   N/A

39. Is the equipment easily understood?   Yes   No   N/A

40. Does elevated equipment provide more than one means of exit of varying degrees of difficulty?   Yes   No   N/A

TUNNEL SLIDE RECOMMENDATIONS

PARK NAME	DATE OF INSPECTION	INSPECTOR

Hazards are apparent from this inspection:

- ❑ Repair the problem,
- ❑ Submit a work order,
- ❑ Barricade or close the area, or
- ❑ Notify your supervisor.
- ❑ _____

TUNNEL SLIDE SAFETY RECOMMENDATIONS

- ❑ No Hazardous Conditions Found
- ❑ Removal/Repair Necessary (Prepare Work Order)

WORK ORDER

Item	Action	Date Completed	Time Spent	Cost ($)

TUNNEL SLIDE ACCESSIBILITY RECOMMENDATIONS

Item	Action	Date Completed	Time Spent	Cost ($)

PARK NAME

DATE OF INSPECTION

INSPECTOR

TYPE OF EQUIPMENT _____

MANUFACTURER _____

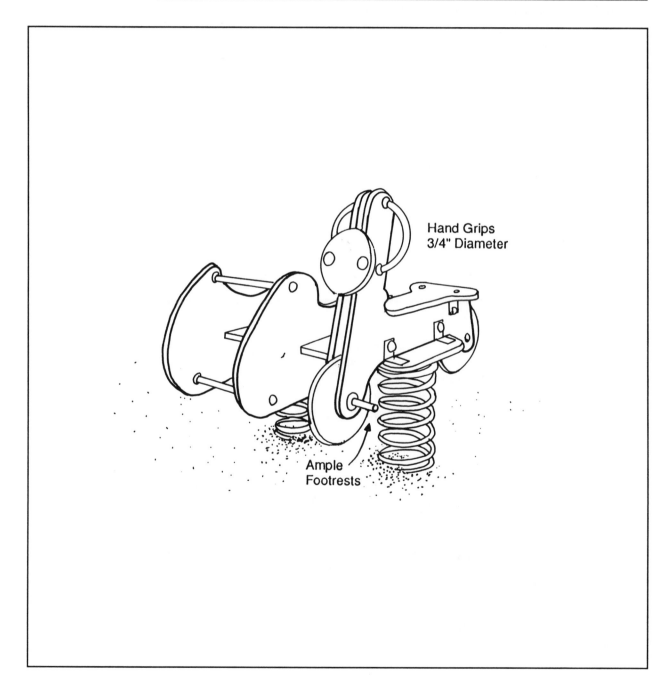

Hand Grips
3/4" Diameter

Ample
Footrests

PARK NAME	DATE OF INSPECTION	INSPECTOR

If any of these items is answered NO, repair/remove the equipment immediately.

EQUIPMENT CONDITION/HEIGHT/FALL ZONE

1. Is the equipment stable and without severe structural deterioration (e.g., at footings and joints)?   Yes   No   N/A

2. Does the equipment have an 6' obstruction-free fall zone?   Yes   No   N/A

ENTRAPMENT

3. Are all openings smaller than 3/8" or greater than 1" to prevent finger entrapment?   Yes   No   N/A

4. Are openings smaller than 3" or larger than 9" to prevent head entrapment?   Yes   No   N/A

5. Are angles greater than 55° to prevent head entrapment?   Yes   No   N/A

GENERAL CONSIDERATIONS

6. Is the equipment complete without missing parts, free of vandalism which would impair safe use, and has no warping or bending of members.   Yes   No   N/A

7. Is the equipment free from pinch or crush points?   Yes   No   N/A

8. Is the equipment free from sharp points, corners, or edges?   Yes   No   N/A

9. Is the equipment free from any protrusions (all nuts and bolts are recessed, fitted with tamper proof locks and the holes plugged)?   Yes   No   N/A

10. Is the equipment free from suspended cables, wires, or ropes which would allow a rapidly moving child to impact his head or neck?   Yes   No   N/A

11. Are the tops of concrete footings buried 12" below the ground level?   Yes   No   N/A

PARK NAME	DATE OF INSPECTION	INSPECTOR

12. Is the scale of the equipment appropriate to the size of the users?   Yes   No   N/A

13. Are the hand grips 3/4" in diameter?   Yes   No   N/A

14. Are ample foot rests provided?   Yes   No   N/A

HARDWARE

15. Is all hardware present, securely attached, and without significant wear or evidence of deformation?   Yes   No   N/A

16. Do fasteners and connecting devices require tools to loosen or remove them (i.e., no hex head bolts or nails are used)?   Yes   No   N/A

17. Are bearings in good condition and well lubricated?   Yes   No   N/A

STRUCTURAL MATERIALS

The structure is made of _____ .

For Wood:

18. Are load bearing members free from rot or insect damage?   Yes   No   N/A

19. Are wood members free from checks more than 24" in length and/or 1/4" in width?   Yes   No   N/A

20. If a wood preservative was used on the structure, list the preservative's name:_____ .

21. Is the wood preservative safe for use in children's play areas?   Yes   No   N/A

22. If a wood preservative was used, has a sealant been applied to treated areas every two years?   Yes   No   N/A

PARK NAME

DATE OF INSPECTION

INSPECTOR

For Metal:

23. If it is steel, is it galvanized or powder coated?   Yes   No   N/A

24. If it is aluminum, is it powder coated or anodized?   Yes   No   N/A

25. Is the equipment free from rust on steel, corrosion on aluminum, or peeling paint?   Yes   No   N/A

For Plastic:

26. Are plastic parts unbroken and without chips or cracks, particularly at joints and connections?   Yes   No   N/A

For Paint:

27. If equipment was painted, was paint without lead used?   Yes   No   N/A

PARK NAME	DATE OF INSPECTION	INSPECTOR

SPRING/ROCKING EQUIPMENT ACCESSIBILITY

28. Is the equipment accessible to individuals with the following disabilities (please check all that apply):   Yes   No   N/A

    ❑ Wheelchair Users   ❑ Cane/Crutch/Walker Users

    ❑ Developmentally Disabled   ❑ Hearing Impaired

    ❑ Visually Impaired   ❑ Emotional/Behavioral Disability

29. Is there a way to make this piece usable by a greater number of people with disabilities? (Please specify.)   Yes   No   N/A

_____

_____

_____

_____

_____

_____

30. Can the equipment be adapted without creating a safety hazard for others?   Yes   No   N/A

31. Can a person using a wheelchair, cane, crutches or other assistive device approach the equipment?   Yes   No   N/A

32. Are clear sight lines provided from the equipment to adult supervision areas?   Yes   No   N/A

33. Is the equipment easily understood?   Yes   No   N/A

SPRING EQUIPMENT RECOMMENDATIONS   22C

PARK NAME

DATE OF INSPECTION

INSPECTOR

Hazards are apparent from this Inspection:

❏ Repair the problem,
❏ Submit a work order,
❏ Barricade or close the area, or
❏ Notify your supervisor.
❏ _____

SPRING/ROCKING EQUIPMENT SAFETY RECOMMENDATIONS

❏ No Hazardous Conditions Found
❏ Removal/Repair Necessary (Prepare Work Order)

WORK ORDER

Item	Action	Date Completed	Time Spent	Cost ($)

SPRING/ROCKING EQUIPMENT ACCESSIBILITY RECOMMENDATIONS

Item	Action	Date Completed	Time Spent	Cost ($)

PARK NAME

DATE OF INSPECTION

INSPECTOR

MANUFACTURER _____.

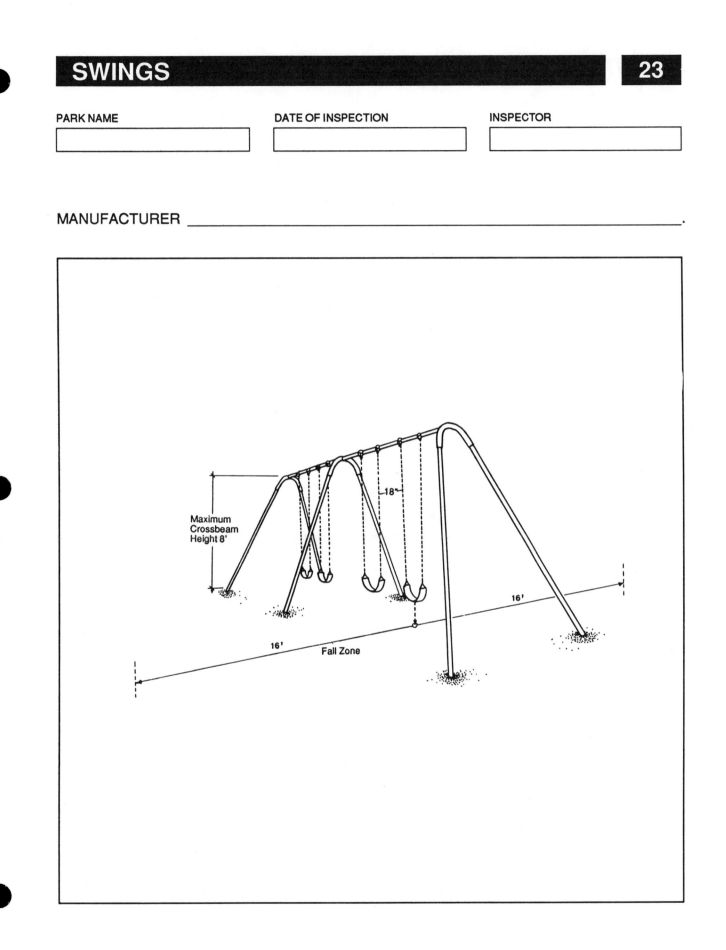

Maximum
Crossbeam
Height 8'

18"

16'

16'

Fall Zone

PARK NAME	DATE OF INSPECTION	INSPECTOR

If any of these items is answered NO, repair/remove the equipment immediately.

EQUIPMENT CONDITION/HEIGHT/FALL ZONE

1. Is the equipment stable and without severe structural deterioration (e.g., at footings and joints)?   Yes   No   N/A

2. Is the swing fall zone (see illustration) two times the height of the swing crossbeam to both the front and back of the equipment (16' in each direction for the 8' maximum crossbeam height)?   Yes   No   N/A

3. Is the swing crossbeam height 8' or less?   Yes   No   N/A

ENTRAPMENT

4. Are all openings smaller than 3/8" or greater than 1" to prevent finger entrapment?   Yes   No   N/A

5. Are openings smaller than 3" or larger than 9" to prevent head entrapment?   Yes   No   N/A

6. Are angles greater than 55° to prevent head entrapment?   Yes   No   N/A

GENERAL CONSIDERATIONS

7. Is the equipment complete without missing parts, free of vandalism which would impair safe use, and has no warping or bending of members.   Yes   No   N/A

8. Are swings hung at least 18" apart?   Yes   No   N/A

9. Can the swing assembly withstand a weight of 1200 lbs. when tested according to the NBS method? (Apply the force at 120° gradually until it reaches 1200 lbs., then hold it for 5 minutes. For information on a testing device contact Paul Hogan, Playground Clearinghouse, 26 Buckwalter Rd., Phoenixville, PA 19460, 215-935-1549.)   Yes   No   N/A

10. Are swings separated from the rest of the playground?   Yes   No   N/A

PARK NAME

DATE OF INSPECTION

INSPECTOR

		Yes	No	N/A
11.	Are swing seats the "slash proof" rubber belt type?	Yes	No	N/A
12.	Is the swing seat free of exposed metal parts or sharp hardware?	Yes	No	N/A
13.	Is the equipment free from pinch or crush points?	Yes	No	N/A
14.	Is the equipment free from sharp points, corners, or edges?	Yes	No	N/A
15.	Is the equipment free from any protrusions (all nuts and bolts are recessed, fitted with tamper proof locks and the holes plugged)?	Yes	No	N/A
16.	Is the equipment free from suspended cables, wires, or ropes which would allow a rapidly moving child to impact his head or neck?	Yes	No	N/A
17.	Are the tops of concrete footings buried 12" below the ground level?	Yes	No	N/A
18.	Is the scale of the equipment appropriate to the size of the users?	Yes	No	N/A

CHAIN

		Yes	No	N/A
19.	Is the chain in good condition without significant wear, especially in the upper 24"?	Yes	No	N/A
20.	Is the chain "proof coil" of 5/0 size with welded links?	Yes	No	N/A

HARDWARE

		Yes	No	N/A
21.	Is all hardware present, securely attached, and without significant wear or evidence of deformation?	Yes	No	N/A
22.	Do fasteners and connecting devices require tools to loosen or remove them (i.e., no hex head bolts or nails are used)?	Yes	No	N/A
23.	Are bearings in good condition and well lubricated?	Yes	No	N/A
24.	Are S-hooks and other connectors fully closed and secure?	Yes	No	N/A

PARK NAME	DATE OF INSPECTION	INSPECTOR

STRUCTURAL MATERIALS

The structure is made of _____.

For Wood:

25. Are load bearing members free from rot or insect damage?   Yes   No   N/A

26. Are wood members free from checks more than 24" in length and/or 1/4" in width?   Yes   No   N/A

27. If a wood preservative was used on the structure, list the preservatives name:_____.

28. Is the wood preservative safe for use in children's play areas?   Yes   No   N/A

29. If a wood preservative was used, has a sealant been applied to treated areas every two years?   Yes   No   N/A

For Metal:

30. If it is steel, is it galvanized or powder coated?   Yes   No   N/A

31. If it is aluminum, is it powder coated or anodized?   Yes   No   N/A

32. Is the equipment free from rust on steel, corrosion on aluminum, or peeling paint?   Yes   No   N/A

For Plastic:

33. Are plastic parts unbroken and without chips or cracks, particularly at joints and connections?   Yes   No   N/A

For Paint:

34. If equipment was painted, was a paint without lead used?   Yes   No   N/A

PARK NAME	DATE OF INSPECTION	INSPECTOR

SWING ACCESSIBILITY

35. Is the equipment accessible to individuals with the following disabilities (please check all that apply):   Yes   No   N/A

   ❑ Wheelchair Users   ❑ Cane/Crutch/Walker Users
   ❑ Developmentally Disabled ❑ Hearing Impaired
   ❑ Visually Impaired   ❑ Emotional/Behavioral Disability

36. Is there a way to make this piece usable by a greater number of people with disabilities? (Please specify.)   Yes   No   N/A

   _____

   _____

   _____

   _____

   _____

   _____

37. Can the equipment be adapted without creating a safety hazard for others?   Yes   No   N/A

38. Can a person using a wheelchair, cane, crutches or other assistive device approach the equipment?   Yes   No   N/A

39. Are clear sight lines provided from the front and back of the equipment and from the equipment to adult supervision areas?   Yes   No   N/A

40. Is the equipment easily understood?   Yes   No   N/A

41. Is there a distinct difference in texture between the swing fall zone and the surrounding area?   Yes   No   N/A

SWING RECOMMENDATIONS

PARK NAME

DATE OF INSPECTION

INSPECTOR

Hazards are apparent from this inspection:

- ❑ Repair the problem,
- ❑ Submit a work order,
- ❑ Barricade or close the area, or
- ❑ Notify your supervisor.
- ❑ _____

SWING SAFETY RECOMMENDATIONS

- ❑ No Hazardous Conditions Found
- ❑ Removal/Repair Necessary (Prepare Work Order)

WORK ORDER

Item	Action	Date Completed	Time Spent	Cost ($)

SWING ACCESSIBILITY RECOMMENDATIONS

Item	Action	Date Completed	Time Spent	Cost ($)

PARK NAME

DATE OF INSPECTION

INSPECTOR

MANUFACTURER _____

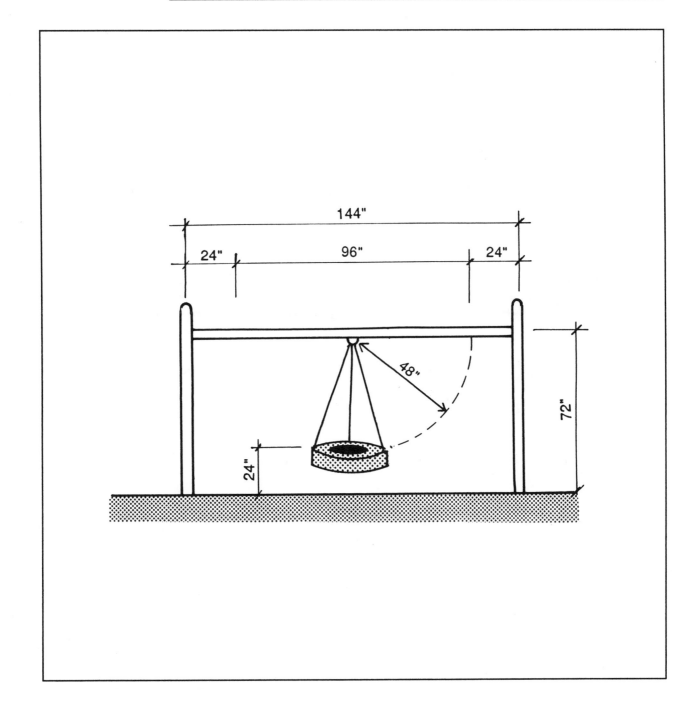

PARK NAME	DATE OF INSPECTION	INSPECTOR

If any of these items is answered NO, repair/remove the equipment immediately.

EQUIPMENT CONDITION/HEIGHT/FALL ZONE

1. Is the equipment stable and without severe structural deterioration (e.g., at footings and joints)? Yes No N/A

2. Is the height of the tire swing 24"? Yes No N/A

3. Is the crossbeam length a minimum of 12' for a standard tire? Yes No N/A

4. Is the weight of the tire 50 pounds or less? Yes No N/A

ENTRAPMENT

5. Are all openings smaller than 3/8" or greater than 1" to prevent finger entrapment? Yes No N/A

6. Are openings smaller than 3" or larger than 9" to prevent head entrapment? Yes No N/A

7. Are angles greater than 55° to prevent head entrapment? Yes No N/A

GENERAL CONSIDERATIONS

8. Is the equipment complete without missing parts, free of vandalism which would impair safe use, and has no warping or bending of members. Yes No N/A

9. Is the equipment free from pinch or crush points? Yes No N/A

10. Is the equipment free from sharp points, corners, or edges? Yes No N/A

11. If the swing is attached to a structure, is the swing attached so that a child cannot easily climb out on the swing beam? Yes No N/A

12. Is the tire swing crossbeam attached to vertical supports on both ends with the swing unit hung at its center? Yes No N/A

PARK NAME	DATE OF INSPECTION	INSPECTOR

13. Is the equipment free from any protrusions (all nuts and bolts are recessed, fitted with tamper proof locks and the holes plugged)?   Yes   No   N/A

14. Is the equipment free from suspended cables, wires, or ropes which would allow a rapidly moving child to impact his head or neck?   Yes   No   N/A

15. Are the tops of concrete footings buried 12" below the ground level?   Yes   No   N/A

16. Is the scale of the equipment appropriate to the size of the users?   Yes   No   N/A

HARDWARE

17. Is all hardware present, securely attached, and without significant wear or evidence of deformation?   Yes   No   N/A

18. Do fasteners and connecting devices require tools to loosen or remove them (i.e., no hex head bolts or nails are used)?   Yes   No   N/A

19. Is the tire swing connected to the crossbeam with a ball joint or a universal joint bearing protected by a boot?   Yes   No   N/A

20. Are joints in good condition, well lubricated and securely attached to the beam?   Yes   No   N/A

21. Are S-hooks and other connectors fully closed and secure?   Yes   No   N/A

CHAIN

22. Is the chain in good condition without significant wear, especially in the upper 24"?   Yes   No   N/A

23. Is the chain "proof coil" of 5/0 size with welded links?   Yes   No   N/A

PARK NAME

DATE OF INSPECTION

INSPECTOR

STRUCTURAL MATERIALS

The structure is made of _____.

For Wood:

24. Are load bearing members free from rot or insect damage?　Yes　No　N/A

25. Are wood members free from checks more than 24" in length and/or 1/4" in width?　Yes　No　N/A

26. If a wood preservative was used on the structure, list the preservative's name:_____.

27. Is the wood preservative safe for use in children's play areas?　Yes　No　N/A

28. If a wood preservative was used, has a sealant been applied to treated areas every two years?　Yes　No　N/A

For Metal:

29. If it is steel, is it galvanized or powder coated?　Yes　No　N/A

30. If it is aluminum, is it powder coated or anodized?　Yes　No　N/A

31. Is the equipment free from rust on steel, corrosion on aluminum, or peeling paint?　Yes　No　N/A

For Plastic:

32. Are plastic parts unbroken and without chips or cracks, particularly at joints and connections?　Yes　No　N/A

For Paint:

33. If equipment was painted, was paint without lead used?　Yes　No　N/A

PARK NAME

DATE OF INSPECTION

INSPECTOR

TIRE SWING ACCESSIBILITY

34. Is the equipment accessible to individuals with the following disabilities (please check all that apply):   Yes   No   N/A

    ❑ Wheelchair Users   ❑ Cane/Crutch/Walker Users

    ❑ Developmentally Disabled   ❑ Hearing Impaired

    ❑ Visually Impaired   ❑ Emotional/Behavioral Disability

35. Is there a way to make this piece usable by a greater number of people with disabilities? (Please specify.)   Yes   No   N/A

_____

_____

_____

_____

_____

_____

36. Can the equipment be adapted without creating a safety hazard for others?   Yes   No   N/A

37. Can a person using a wheelchair, cane, crutches or other assistive device approach the equipment?   Yes   No   N/A

38. Are clear sight lines provided from the front and back of the equipment and from the equipment to adult supervision areas?   Yes   No   N/A

39. Is the equipment easily understood?   Yes   No   N/A

40. Is there a distinct difference in texture between the swing fall zone and the surrounding area?   Yes   No   N/A

PARK NAME

DATE OF INSPECTION

INSPECTOR

Hazards are apparent from this inspection:

❑ Repair the problem,
❑ Submit a work order,
❑ Barricade or close the area, or
❑ Notify your supervisor.
❑ _____

TIRE SWING SAFETY RECOMMENDATIONS

❑ No Hazardous Conditions Found
❑ Removal/Repair Necessary (Prepare Work Order)

WORK ORDER

Item	Action	Date Completed	Time Spent	Cost ($)

TIRE SWING ACCESSIBILITY RECOMMENDATIONS

Item	Action	Date Completed	Time Spent	Cost ($)

PARK NAME

DATE OF INSPECTION

INSPECTOR

MANUFACTURER _____

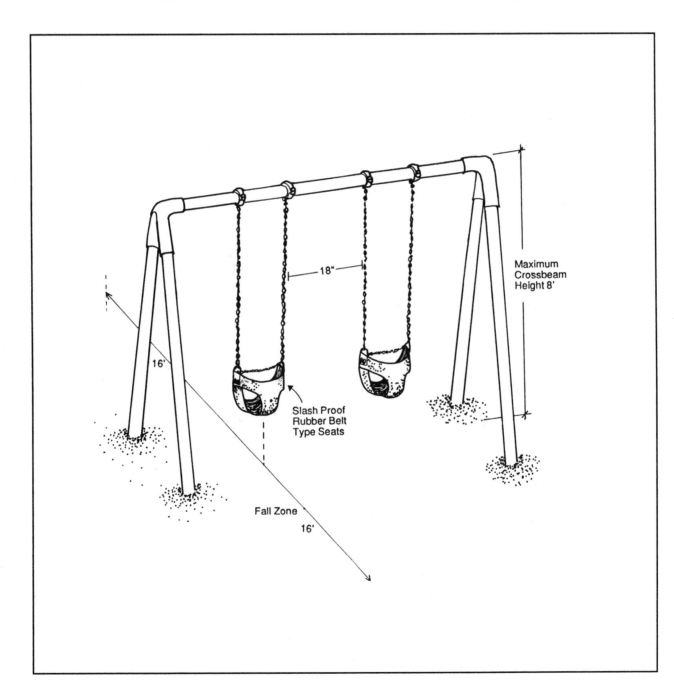

18"

Maximum
Crossbeam
Height 8'

16'

Slash Proof
Rubber Belt
Type Seats

Fall Zone
16'

PARK NAME	DATE OF INSPECTION	INSPECTOR

If any of these items is answered NO, repair/remove the equipment immediately.

EQUIPMENT CONDITION/HEIGHT/FALL ZONE

1. Is the equipment stable and without severe structural deterioration (e.g., at footings and joints)?   Yes   No   N/A

2. Is the swing fall zone (see illustration) two times the height of the swing crossbeam to both the front and back of the equipment (16' in each direction for the 8' maximum crossbeam height)?   Yes   No   N/A

3. Is the swing crossbeam height 8' or less?   Yes   No   N/A

ENTRAPMENT

4. Are all openings smaller than 3/8" or greater than 1" to prevent finger entrapment?   Yes   No   N/A

5. Are openings smaller than 3" or larger than 9" to prevent head entrapment?   Yes   No   N/A

6. Are angles greater than 55° to prevent head entrapment?   Yes   No   N/A

GENERAL CONSIDERATIONS

7. Is the equipment complete without missing parts, free of vandalism which would impair safe use, and has no warping or bending of members.   Yes   No   N/A

8. Are the swings hung at least 18" apart?   Yes   No   N/A

9. Can the assembly withstand a weight of 1200 lbs. when tested according to the NBS method? (Apply the force at 120° gradually until it reaches 1200 lbs., then hold it for 5 minutes. For information on a testing device, contact Paul Hogan, Playground Clearinghouse, 26 Buckwalter Rd., Phoenixville, PA 19460, 215-935-1549.)   Yes   No   N/A

10. Are swings separated from the rest of the playground?   Yes   No   N/A

PARK NAME

DATE OF INSPECTION

INSPECTOR

11. Is the tot swing seat the soft rubber belt type?   Yes   No   N/A

12. Is the swing seat free of exposed metal parts or sharp   Yes   No   N/A
    hardware?

13. Is the equipment free from pinch or crush points?   Yes   No   N/A

14. Is the equipment free from any protrusions (all nuts and   Yes   No   N/A
    bolts are recessed, fitted with tamper proof locks and the
    holes plugged)?

15. Are the tops of concrete footings buried 12" below the   Yes   No   N/A
    ground level?

16. Is the equipment free from suspended cables, wires, or   Yes   No   N/A
    ropes which would allow a rapidly moving child to impact
    his head or neck?

17. Is the scale of the equipment appropriate to the size of the users?   Yes   No   N/A

CHAIN

18. Is the chain in good condition without significant wear,   Yes   No   N/A
    especially in the upper 24"?

19. Is the chain "proof coil" of 5/0 size with welded links?   Yes   No   N/A

HARDWARE

20. Is all hardware present, securely attached, and without   Yes   No   N/A
    significant wear or evidence of deformation?

21. Do fasteners and connecting devices require tools to   Yes   No   N/A
    loosen or remove them (i.e., no hex head bolts or nails are
    used)?

22. Are bearings in good condition and well lubricated?   Yes   No   N/A

23. Are S-hooks and other connectors fully closed and secure?   Yes   No   N/A

PARK NAME

DATE OF INSPECTION

INSPECTOR

STRUCTURAL MATERIALS

The structure is made of _____ .

For Wood:

24. Are load bearing members free from rot or insect damage?   Yes   No   N/A

25. Are wood members free from checks more than 24" in length and/or 1/4" in width?   Yes   No   N/A

26. If a wood preservative was used on the structure, list the preservatives name:_____ .

27. Is the wood preservative safe for use in children's play areas?   Yes   No   N/A

28. If a wood preservative was used, has a sealant been applied to treated areas every two years?   Yes   No   N/A

For Metal:

29. If it is steel, is it galvanized or powder coated?   Yes   No   N/A

30. If it is aluminum, is it powder coated or anodized?   Yes   No   N/A

31. Is the equipment free from rust on steel, corrosion on aluminum, or peeling paint?   Yes   No   N/A

For Plastic:

32. Are plastic parts unbroken and without chips or cracks, particularly at joints and connections?   Yes   No   N/A

For Paint:

33. If equipment was painted, was paint without lead used?   Yes   No   N/A

PARK NAME	DATE OF INSPECTION	INSPECTOR

TOT SWING ACCESSIBILITY

34. Is the equipment accessible to individuals with the following disabilities (please check all that apply):

   Yes   No   N/A

   ❑ Wheelchair Users   ❑ Cane/Crutch/Walker Users
   ❑ Developmentally Disabled   ❑ Hearing Impaired
   ❑ Visually Impaired   ❑ Emotional/Behavioral Disability

35. Is there a way to make this piece usable by a greater number of people with disabilities? (Please specify.)

   Yes   No   N/A

   _____

   _____

   _____

   _____

   _____

36. Can the equipment be adapted without creating a safety hazard for others?

   Yes   No   N/A

37. Can a person using a wheelchair, cane, crutches or other assistive device approach the equipment?

   Yes   No   N/A

38. Are clear sight lines provided from the front and back of the equipment and from the equipment to adult supervision areas?

   Yes   No   N/A

39. Is the equipment easily understood?

   Yes   No   N/A

40. Is there a distinct transition to area either in texture between the swing fall zone and the surrounding area or a defined barrier?

   Yes   No   N/A

PARK NAME

DATE OF INSPECTION

INSPECTOR

Hazards are apparent from this inspection:

❏ Repair the problem,
❏ Submit a work order,
❏ Barricade or close the area, or
❏ Notify your supervisor.
❏ _____

TOT SWING SAFETY RECOMMENDATIONS

❏ No Hazardous Conditions Found
❏ Removal/Repair Necessary (Prepare Work Order)

WORK ORDER

Item	Action	Date Completed	Time Spent	Cost ($)

TOT SWING ACCESSIBILITY RECOMMENDATIONS

Item	Action	Date Completed	Time Spent	Cost ($)

PARK NAME

DATE OF INSPECTION

INSPECTOR

TYPE OF TUNNEL _____

MANUFACTURER _____

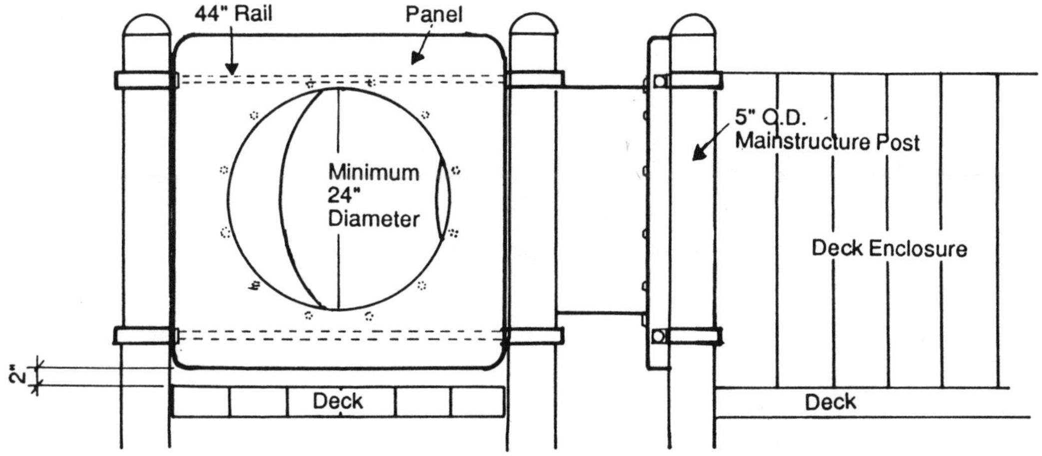

44" Rail   Panel

Minimum
24"
Diameter

5" O.D.
Mainstructure Post

Deck Enclosure

2"

Deck   Deck

PARK NAME	DATE OF INSPECTION	INSPECTOR

If any of these items is answered NO, repair/remove the equipment immediately.

EQUIPMENT CONDITION/HEIGHT/FALL ZONE

1. Is the equipment stable and without severe structural deterioration (e.g., at footings and joints)?   Yes   No   N/A

2. Does the equipment have an 8' obstruction-free fall zone?   Yes   No   N/A

3. Are all tunnel edges rounded?   Yes   No   N/A

4. Is the interior diameter at least 24"?   Yes   No   N/A

ENTRAPMENT

5. Are all openings smaller than 3/8" or greater than 1" to prevent finger entrapment?   Yes   No   N/A

6. Are openings smaller than 3" or larger than 9" to prevent head entrapment?   Yes   No   N/A

7. Are angles greater than 55° to prevent head entrapment?   Yes   No   N/A

GENERAL CONSIDERATIONS

8. Is the equipment complete without missing parts, free of vandalism which would impair safe use, and has no warping or bending of members.   Yes   No   N/A

9. Is the equipment free from pinch or crush points?   Yes   No   N/A

10. Is the equipment free from sharp points, corners, or edges?   Yes   No   N/A

11. Is the equipment free from any protrusions (all nuts and bolts are recessed, fitted with tamper proof locks and the holes plugged)?   Yes   No   N/A

PARK NAME

DATE OF INSPECTION

INSPECTOR

12. Is the equipment free from suspended cables, wires, or ropes which would allow a rapidly moving child to impact his head or neck?　　Yes　　No　　N/A

13. Are all platforms above 30" surrounded by non-climbable protective barriers at least 38" in height?　　Yes　　No　　N/A

14. Are the tops of concrete footings buried 12" below the ground level?　　Yes　　No　　N/A

15. Is the scale of the equipment appropriate to the size of the users?　　Yes　　No　　N/A

HARDWARE

16. Is all hardware present, securely attached, and without significant wear or evidence of deformation?　　Yes　　No　　N/A

17. Do fasteners and connecting devices require tools to loosen or remove them (i.e., no hex head bolts or nails are used)?　　Yes　　No　　N/A

STRUCTURAL MATERIALS

The structure is made of _____ .
(Concrete is not acceptable.)

For Wood:

18. Are load bearing members free from rot or insect damage?　　Yes　　No　　N/A

19. Are wood members free from checks more than 24" in length and/or 1/4" in width?　　Yes　　No　　N/A

20. If a wood preservative was used on the structure, list the preservatives name:_____ .

PARK NAME

DATE OF INSPECTION

INSPECTOR

21. Is the wood preservative safe for use in children's play areas?　　Yes　No　N/A

22. If a wood preservative was used, has a sealant been applied to treated areas every two years?　　Yes　No　N/A

For Metal:

23. If it is steel, is it galvanized or powder coated?　　Yes　No　N/A

24. If it is aluminum, is it powder coated or anodized?　　Yes　No　N/A

25. Is the equipment free from rust on steel, corrosion on aluminum, or peeling paint?　　Yes　No　N/A

For Plastic:

26. Are plastic parts unbroken and without chips or cracks, particularly at joints and connections?　　Yes　No　N/A

For Paint:

27. If equipment was painted, was paint without lead used?　　Yes　No　N/A

PARK NAME | DATE OF INSPECTION | INSPECTOR

TUNNEL ACCESSIBILITY

28. Is the equipment accessible to individuals with the following disabilities (please check all that apply):   Yes   No   N/A

- ❏ Wheelchair Users
- ❏ Developmentally Disabled
- ❏ Visually Impaired
- ❏ Cane/Crutch/Walker Users
- ❏ Hearing Impaired
- ❏ Emotional/Behavioral Disability

29. Is there a way to make this piece usable by a greater number of people with disabilities? (Please specify.)   Yes   No   N/A

_____

_____

_____

_____

_____

_____

30. Can the equipment be adapted without creating a safety hazard for others?   Yes   No   N/A

31. Can a person using a wheelchair, cane, crutches or other assistive device approach the equipment?   Yes   No   N/A

32. Are clear sight lines provided from the top to the bottom of the equipment and from the equipment to adult supervision areas?   Yes   No   N/A

33. Is the equipment easily understood?   Yes   No   N/A

34. Does elevated equipment provide more than one means of exit of varying degrees of difficulty?   Yes   No   N/A

TUNNEL RECOMMENDATIONS

PARK NAME

DATE OF INSPECTION

INSPECTOR

Hazards are apparent from this inspection:

❑ Repair the problem,
❑ Submit a work order,
❑ Barricade or close the area, or
❑ Notify your supervisor.
❑ _____

TUNNEL SAFETY RECOMMENDATIONS

❑ No Hazardous Conditions Found
❑ Removal/Repair Necessary (Prepare Work Order)

WORK ORDER

Item	Action	Date Completed	Time Spent	Cost ($)

TUNNEL ACCESSIBILITY RECOMMENDATIONS

Item	Action	Date Completed	Time Spent	Cost ($)

SELECTED BIBLIOGRAPHY

Adaptive Environments Center (1980). Environments for All Children. *Access Information Bulletin.* Washington, DC: NCBFE.

ASTM (1986). F-355/86. Standard Test Method for Shock- Absorbing Properties of Play Surface Systems and Materials.

Barrier Free Environments, Inc. (1980). Doors and Entrances. *Access Information Bulletin.* Washington, DC: NCBFE.

Beamish, A. (1980). Child–Pedestrian Safety in Residential Environments. Ottawa: CMHC.

Björklid, P. (1984–85). Environmental Diversity on Housing Estates as a Factor in Child Development. *Children's Environmental Quarterly.* 1(4), 7–13.

Blakely, K. (Ed.) (1985). Safety in Outdoor Play. Special issue of *Children's Environments Quarterly.* 2(4), Winter 1985.

Boyce, W.T., Sobolewski, S., Sprunger, L., & Schaefer, C. (1984). Playground Equipment Injuries in a Large, Urban School District. *American Journal of Public Health.* 74:9, 984–6.

British Standard Institute. (1979). BS5696 Play Equipment Intended for Permanent Installation Outdoors. London: BSI.

Bruya, L.D. (1988). *Play Spaces for Children: A New Beginning: Vol. II.* Reston, VA. American Alliance for Health, Physical Education, Recreation and Dance.

Bruya, L.D., and Langendorfer, S.J. (1988). *Where Our Children Play: Elementary School Playground Equipment, Vol. I.* Reston, VA: American Alliance for Health, Physical Education, Recreation and Dance.

Bunin, N., Jasperse, D., & Cooper, S. (1980). *A Guide to Designing Accessible Outdoor Recreation Facilities.* Washington, DC: U.S. Dept. of the Interior, Heritage, Recreation and Conservation Service (Lake Central Regional Office, Ann Arbor, MI).

City of Seattle, Department of Parks and Recreation (1986). *Guidelines for Play Areas: Recommendations for Planning, Design and Maintenance.* Seattle, WA: Department of Parks and Recreation.

Esbensen, S.B. (1979). An International Inventory and Comparative Study of Legislation and Guidelines for Children's Play Spaces in the Residential Environment. Ottawa: CMHC.

Fair Play for Children (n.d.). *Safety Checklist.* London: FPC and NPFA.

Freedberg, L. (1983). *America's Poisoned Playgrounds: Children and Toxic Chemicals.* Oakland: Youth News.

General Services Administration (1988). *Uniform Federal Accessibility Standards, Federal Standard 795.* Washington D.C.:U.S. Government Printing Office.

Gold, S.M. (1981). Designing Public Playgrounds for User Safety. *Australian Parks and Recreation.* 22:3, 10–14.

– – –. (1988). Safety Checklists for Parks and Recreation Areas. *Proceedings of the California Park and Recreation Society Conference* in Long Beach, California.

SELECTED BIBLIOGRAPHY

– – –. (1988). Playground Design: The Standard of Care. *California Council of Landscape Architects Quarterly.*

Harkness, S. & Groom, J. (1976). Building without Barriers for the Disabled. NY: Watson-Guptill Publications.

Jeavons, S. (1987). Criteria for Assessment of Play Environments. *Australian Parks and Recreation.* 23(2), 7–13.

King, F. (1980). *Towards a Safer Adventure Playground.* London: NPFA.

Kompan (1984). *Playgrounds and Safety: Comparison Between Various Playground Equipment Standards.* Windsor Locks, CT: Kompan.

Moore, R.C., Goltsman, S.M. & Iacofano, D.S. (1987). *PLAY FOR ALL Guidelines: Planning, Design and Management of Outdoor Play Settings for All Children.* Berkeley, CA: MIG Communications.

National Safety Council. (1985). *Accident Facts: 1985 Edition.* Chicago: National Safety Council (444 N. Michigan Ave., Chicago, IL 60611).

Nordhaus, R.S., Kantrowitz, M. & Siembieda, W.J. (1984). *Accessible Fishing: A Planning Handbook.* Santa Fe, NM: New Mexico Natural Resources Dept.

Peoples Housing, Inc. (1983). *Retrofitting Public Restrooms for Accessibility.* Sacramento, CA: California Department of Rehabilitation.

Root, J. (1983). *Play Without Pain.* Melbourne: Child Accident Prevention Foundation of Australia.

Sandels, S. (1968). *Children in Traffic.* London: Paul Elek.

Schneekloth, L. (1985). *Play Environments for Disabled Children: Design Guidelines.* Unpublished ms.

– – –. (1974). *Environments for Visually Impaired Children: Design Guidelines.* College of Architecture, Virginia Polytechnic Institute and State University, Blacksburg, VA. Unpublished ms.

Standards Association of New Zealand (1986). *NZS 5828: Part 1: General Guidelines for New and Existing Playgrounds – Equipment and Surfacing.* Wellington, New Zealand: Standards Association.

U.S. Consumer Product Safety Commission. (1981) *A Handbook for Public Playground Safety. Vol I: General Guidelines for New and Existing Playgrounds. Vol II: Technical Guidelines for Equipment and Surfacing.* Washington, DC: CPSC.

EVALUATION

Thank you for purchasing the *Safety First Checklist!*

We will be updating this edition periodically to include new research to better meet the needs of park safety and maintenance staff.

Please use the space below to send us your comments, ideas for revisions and/or user experiences.

Return to: PLAY FOR ALL Safety First Checklist, 1802 Fifth Street, Berkeley, CA 94710